DEAR GRAHAM,

ON BEHALF OF BRITISH AIRWAYS WE
WOULD LIKE TO THANK YOU FOR YOUR
43 YEARS SERVICE. FROM YOUR APPRENTICE
DAYS AT BEA, TO THE ENGINE WORKSHOP
IN TBD AND FINALLY YOUR TIME IN CABIN
DESIGN. IT HAS BEEN A PLEASURE WORKING
WITH YOU.

KIND REGARDS,

FROM YOUR FRIENDS & COLLEAGUES

British Aviation Posters

Art, Design and Flight

Imperial Airways

and Associated Companies

Operate the world's longest air route

THE SERVICES FROM JOHANNESBURG TO CAPE TOWN ARE NOW OPERATED BY SOUTH AFRICAN AIRWAYS.

PRINTED IN ENGLAND BY M'CORQUODALE & CO. LTD, LONDON, AND PUBLISHED IN GREAT BRITAIN BY IMPERIAL AIRWAYS LTD, LONDON.

British Aviation Posters

Art, Design and Flight

SCOTT ANTHONY AND OLIVER GREEN

Lund Humphries in association with British Airways

First published in 2012 by Lund Humphries in association with British Airways

BRITISH AIRWAYS

Lund Humphries
Wey Court East
Union Road
Farnham
Surrey GU9 7PT
UK

Lund Humphries
Suite 420
101 Cherry Street
Burlington
VT 05401-4405
USA

www.lundhumphries.com

Lund Humphries is part of Ashgate Publishing

British Library Cataloguing in Publication Data

Anthony, Scott, 1977-
  British aviation posters : art, design and flight.
  1. British Airways--Posters. 2. Imperial Airways--
  Posters. 3. Travel posters, British--20th century.
  4. Aeronautics, Commercial--Great Britain--Marketing--
  History--20th century.
  I. Title II. Green, Oliver.
  741.6'74'0941'0904-dc23

ISBN: 9781848220843

Library of Congress Control Number: 2012930112

Edited by Howard Watson
Designed by Heather Bowen

Printed in Slovenia

Frontispiece:
Imperial Airways operate the world's longest air route
Unknown designer
Imperial Airways poster, 1936

Contents

Introduction

The Art of Speedbird

OLIVER GREEN AND SCOTT ANTHONY

This book came about through our introduction to a remarkable collection of posters in the archives of British Airways (BA). These graphic images, produced to publicise and promote BA's five principal predecessors, Imperial Airways, British Airways Limited, BOAC, BEA and BSAA, cover a wide range of artistic styles from the golden age of poster design. The posters from the 1930s are particularly striking, dating from a period of less than ten years when Imperial's publicity was expertly managed by the Stuarts advertising agency under Marcus Brumwell. Stuarts was a go-ahead agency that immediately took Imperial and its rather stuffy, conservative image in hand. Brumwell was soon commissioning some of the most creative artists, designers and illustrators of the period including Edward Bawden, James Gardner, Edward McKnight Kauffer, Theyre Lee-Elliott, Ben Nicholson, John Piper and Rex Whistler.

Imperial and Stuarts took their cue from the companies and organisations that had begun to set new standards in British advertising, publicity and commercial design in the 1920s, notably the London Underground, London & North Eastern

Railway (LNER), Empire Marketing Board (EMB) and Shell Oil. The publicity managers of these outfits – Frank Pick at the Underground, William Teasdale and Cecil Dandridge at the LNER, Stephen Tallents, first at the EMB then at the Post Office, and Jack Beddington at Shell – all knew that they were selling dreams and ideas, not tickets or tins of beans, and their creative campaigns were stylish and compelling.

As a newcomer created in 1924, Imperial Airways spent its early years struggling with the basic practicalities of building a civil aviation industry for Britain where none had existed before. It was starting from scratch, seriously under-resourced and facing technological and logistical challenges that required considerable research and development. Aviation was still at a fairly primitive stage, and progress was both hindered and encouraged by intense international competition to be the first or best in a particular field. Governments were uncertain about which projects to back and national policies were inconsistent. Change was sometimes determined by fate not design, such as the decision to abandon airship development in Britain after the

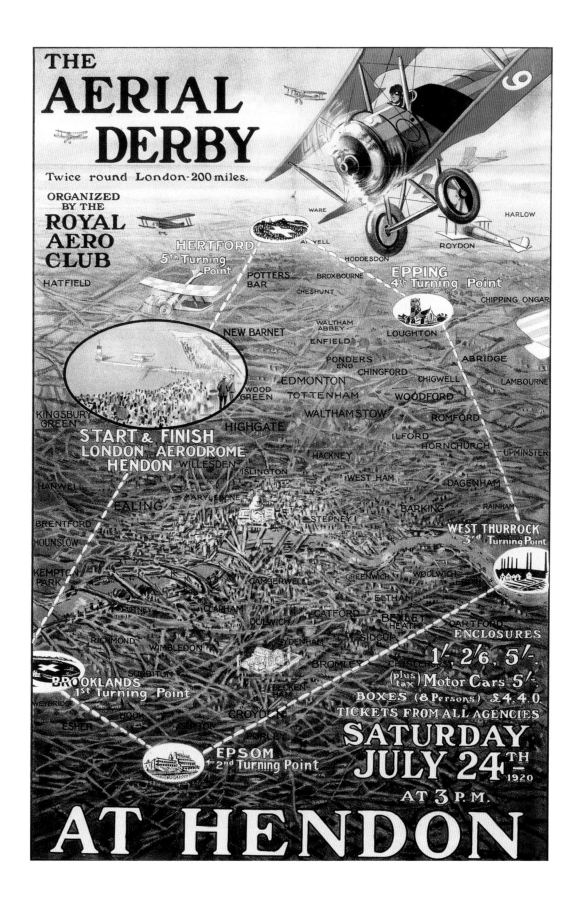

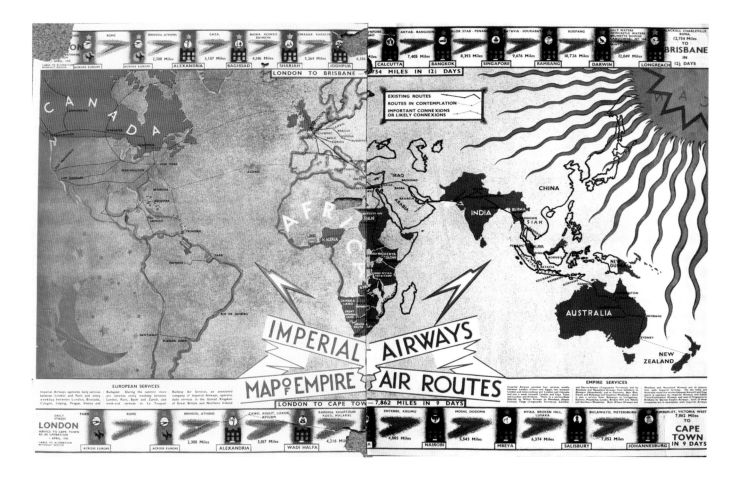

**3 Imperial Airways Map
of Empire Air Routes**
Unknown designer
Imperial Airways poster, c.1937

R101 disaster in 1930, when a newly built British airship crashed in France on its maiden voyage to India, killing nearly everybody on board.

The arrival of Bill Snowden Gamble as publicity manager for Imperial Airways in 1931, and his appointment of Stuarts as its advertising agency, was a turning point for the airline because it began to take marketing and publicity seriously for the first time. Poster design was a key part of a new strategy that soon included print publicity, the design of a distinctive company symbol – the famous Speedbird – and the embracing of the new

visual medium of sound film. It also involved close cooperation with key partner organisations, notably the General Post Office over the promotion of the airmail programme, and major suppliers such as Shell, which was already an expert image-builder with a reputation for artistic patronage that put it well ahead of its rivals.

These organisations saw the opportunity to work together for mutual benefit. The result was an extraordinary burst of managed creativity where a wide range of artists, designers and film-makers became involved in the promotion of civil

4 **Travel Comfortably**
Designer: Fougasse
(Cyril Kenneth Bird)
Imperial Airways poster, 1936

The winged waiter has recently
reappeared on BA's first class
in-flight menus.

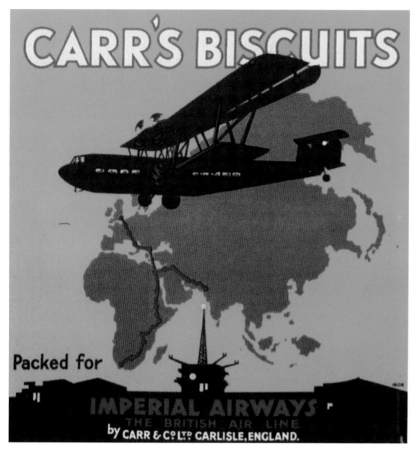

5 A Carr's biscuit label used for product promotion in early airline catering. It reproduces an original Imperial Airways poster by an unknown designer featuring an HP42 airliner used on the main Empire routes through Asia and Africa in the 1930s.

6 *The Golden Picture Book of Aeroplanes*
Cover designer: Gildersleve for BEA, published by Ward Lock, 1953

The illustration shows a BEA Viking flying over St Paul's cathedral and the bomb-damaged City of London.

aviation and the national carrier. At the end of the 1930s, Imperial's passenger numbers were still tiny compared with airline patronage today but the whole nation, including the dominions of the British Empire, was able to feel part of something that was linked around the world by Speedbird and Air Mail. In a sense everyone in Britain had become, as Sir Alan Cobham liked to put it at the time, 'air minded', even if they had never flown themselves.

In April 1940 Imperial Airways and British Airways Ltd merged to form the British Overseas Airways Corporation (BOAC) but normal civil aviation had already been suspended because of the Second World War. Six years later, BOAC began peacetime operations alongside two new state airlines, British European Airways (BEA) and the

short-lived British South American Airways (BSAA). Despite the austerity there was a second period of quality design promotion in the period from the late 1940s to the early 1960s. This expanded further from poster and print publicity to an all-encompassing strategy covering every aspect of industrial design and corporate identity. It featured the work of designers like Robin Day, Mary de Saulles and Gaby Schreiber as well as graphic artists like Abram Games and F.H.K. Henrion. In the jet age the new media of television and colour magazines gradually took over from posters and traditional printed publicity as the prime promotional mode for aviation in a wealthier consumer society. Design standards fell, the narrative changed and we leave the story of aviation in this country since the 1960s – the years

7 BOAC Constellation
Speedbird publicity postcard,
c.1950

These graceful American
airliners were used on long
distance post-war services from
1946 and given the new white,
blue and silver BOAC livery.

8 British Empire Flying Boat
Unknown designer
Imperial Airways poster, c.1937
The text and captions are
in Dutch.

B.O.A.C. Constellation Speedbird

of Concorde, the new British Airways and mass
market flying – to others.

We are not art, design or aviation historians,
and although we have made extensive use of many
excellent studies in these areas, our intention was
to explore how posters, publicity and design reflected
the broader social history and cultural impact of
civil aviation in twentieth-century Britain. We start
with a look back at the pioneers of flight before
civil aviation had begun, follow the roller-coaster
developments and difficulties that arose between
the 1920s and the 1960s, and end with a postscript
to the first jet age.

Watervliegtuig der Britsche Lijnen—28 in aanbouw
lengte 26 m. 80 • hoogte vanaf de waterlijn 7 m. 30 • snelheid 320 Km. per uur
vleugelwijdte 35 m. gewicht, geheel bevracht • ongeveer 18 ton •

IMPERIAL AIRWAYS
EUROPA • AFRIKA • INDIË • HET VERRE OOSTEN • AUSTRALIË

9 Fly by BOAC
Designer: Dick Negus
and Philip Sharland
BOAC poster, 1954

Taking to the Air:
From Pioneers to Imperial

OLIVER GREEN

Air Pioneers

In the early years of the twentieth century, aviation was an entirely new field, a world of pioneers, dreamers and eccentrics working outside the mainstream of everyday life. In 1903 the Wright brothers[1] famously succeeded in making the first, brief, powered flight at Kitty Hawk, North Carolina, in the United States. At the same time other individual inventors and experimenters in Europe and North America were working independently to develop flying machines, with varying degrees of success.

Flight had long been possible by balloon, of course, and both man-lifting kites and airships were under development by the turn of the century. The theoretical possibility of powered flight had been calculated in the mid-Victorian period by the English aristocrat Sir George Cayley,[2] who experimented with gliders but did not have a suitable power source available. It was not until the early 1900s that the Wrights and others were able to prove that powered and controllable aviation by aircraft was realistic and achievable.

Yet despite the exciting possibilities this raised, aviation development remained fragmented and small scale in Britain and elsewhere. It continued to be a cottage industry where primitive and curious-looking flying machines were put together by engineers and mechanics in small workshops and under railway arches.

Popular Edwardian science-fiction writers like H.G. Wells and F.S. Brereton foresaw the development of planes, rockets and other futuristic aircraft for both military and peaceful purposes, often imaginatively described and illustrated in their books.[3] Progress towards the realisation of such ideas came more slowly, usually through the encouragement or backing of wealthy individuals rather than any enthusiasm or interest from politicians or governments.

Lord Northcliffe,[4] owner and publisher of the *Daily Mail*, was a leading advocate and enthusiast for new technology of all kinds and aviation in particular. It was his newspaper that offered a cash prize to the first person to fly the English Channel, won by the French airman Louis Blériot (1872–1936) in 1909. This was a seminal moment because it was the first demonstration of practical powered flight from one country to

another across the sea. But this advance could be taken two ways: Northcliffe was worried about possible invasion by air and H.G. Wells warned, 'we are no longer, from a military point of view, an inaccessible island';[5] others saw it as breaking down national barriers. The Swiss architect Le Corbusier recalled many years later that his then employer, the French architect Auguste Perret (1874–1954), had burst into their Paris offices brandishing a newspaper and exclaiming, 'Blériot has crossed the Channel! Wars are finished: no more wars are possible! There are no longer any frontiers!'[6]

In fact, some military authorities now began to take the aeroplane seriously as a potential weapon of war for the first time. In 1910 the first International Conference for Aerial Navigation (ICAN) debated issues relating to the sovereignty of the air. Germany professed interest in promoting the freedom of the skies while the British government opposed this view, preferring to protect the air space above the UK as the sole reserve of British pilots. The British Air Navigation Acts of 1911 and 1913 seemed devised to protect Britain *against* aviation rather than to promote it. This attitude set the tone for a competitive and combative approach instead of a cooperative internationalist strategy between different countries when civil aviation was eventually developed in Europe after the First World War.

Meanwhile early air shows in Britain developed a similar atmosphere to the first motor racing events, which also took place in the Edwardian era and often at the same venues. At Brooklands, near Weybridge in Surrey, the world's first purpose-built motorsport circuit was opened in 1907. A year later the early flight trials of one of the first British built powered aircraft took place there, piloted by Alliott Verdon-Roe, whose

Avro company was to become a leading plane manufacturer. Britain's first flying school opened at Brooklands in 1910, run by Hilda Hewlett and French aviator Gustave Blondeau. Mrs Hewlett was the first woman in Britain to hold a pilot's certificate from the Royal Aero Club. T.O.M. ('Tommy') Sopwith,[7] another pioneer aircraft designer, had his first flight with Blondeau at Brooklands.

In many cases air displays had all the razzmatazz of a circus or travelling show, and the aviators themselves were sometimes both pioneers and showmen. The best known of these characters in Edwardian England was a flamboyant American called Samuel Franklin Cody (1867–1913). His popular theatrical acts and demonstrations in Britain and Europe included sharp-shooting, horse-riding, cycle-racing and elaborate man-lifting kites he had designed himself.

In 1907 Cody worked with a British Army team at Aldershot on the *Nulli Secundus* (Latin for 'second to none'), England's first powered airship. At the same time he started building another machine known as 'British Army Aeroplane no.1'. Cody first took to the air in this at Farnborough on 5 October 1908 and entered the record books. Despite his achievement, the Army lost interest in the project and ended his contract, leaving him to continue his aircraft development without official funding.

Cody died in August 1913 when he was thrown to the ground from his latest plane after it broke up mysteriously when he was flying at about 500 feet. He was buried with full military honours and a crowd of 10,000 people were said to have lined the route of the funeral procession to Aldershot military cemetery. 'I have done very little to shout about,' he had once remarked, 'but still, I have accomplished one thing that I hoped for very much,

that is, to be the first man to fly in Great Britain.'[8]

The first aerodrome for London was established in 1910 7 miles (11.3 km) north-west of Charing Cross at Hendon. The rural site, just outside the urban area, was acquired and turned into an airfield and aviation centre by Claude Grahame-White,[9] who built and raced planes there. The Hampstead Tube (officially known as the Charing Cross, Euston and Hampstead Railway, precursor to the Northern line) had opened from central London to nearby Golders Green in 1907, and weekend bus trips to Hendon from the tube terminus were soon on offer. In 1912, when the first aerial derby was held at Hendon, at least 45,000 people paid for admission to the enclosures and thousands more got their first sight of an aircraft as the competitors flew over north London. The mass spectacle of flight had begun, although full participation was limited.

New transport technology gave city dwellers the means and the opportunity to visit the countryside easily and cheaply in their leisure time, and Hendon became a popular new venue for holiday excursions. Frank Pick,[10] the Commercial Manager of the London Underground, was already building a reputation for effective publicity through striking pictorial posters for the tube and buses at this time. In 1913, and again the following year, Pick commissioned posters promoting 'Flying at Hendon' from illustrator Tony Sarg,[11] whose designs vividly convey the drama and activity at London's latest attraction. From 1909 there was a big indoor aviation show each year in the Great Hall at Kensington Olympia, which was also promoted annually with an Underground poster.

Commercial prospects for aviation still looked poor at this stage, and early air shows and exhibitions were treated as spectator events for the general public rather than serious demonstrations of the future possibilities of flying. Colourful lithographic posters were already becoming the standard way to advertise such events and were often commissioned by the railway companies, who in turn offered special excursion rates to attend the shows.

Two major flying events in Doncaster and Blackpool in October 1909 each claimed to be offering England's first aviation races, and both were advertised on railway posters. In fact, neither of these pioneer events was very well attended because of poor weather conditions and they did little to enhance public interest in flying. As a spectator sport, aviation meets seemed unlikely to supersede horse-racing.

Early aircraft lacked the speed, carrying capacity and reliability necessary for successful commercial operation. All of them were still primitive and could not be guaranteed to reach even a close destination. Grahame-White, attempting to make the first experimental airmail flight in 1910 along the Lancashire coast between Blackpool and Southport, was forced down after just 7 miles (11.3 km) by bad weather.[12]

The first successful demonstration of goods transport by air appears to have been the unlikely combination of a French aviator flying a British-built aircraft in India. On 18 February 1911 Henri Pequet (1888–1974), using a Humber bi-plane, flew a small parcel of mail from Allahabad to Naini in connection with the United Provinces Exhibition. Airmail philatelists accept this as the world's first postal delivery by air.

In September of the same year the Grahame-White Aviation Company operated a series of flights from Hendon to Windsor to commemorate the coronation of King George V. Over a three-week period, using French Farman and Blériot machines, Grahame-White's pilots delivered over 26,000 letters and 97,000 postcards to Windsor

Castle. The 'service' was short-lived but it was an impressive demonstration of how aircraft might be used to speed up the mail in the future. It was widely regarded at the time as a stunt, but the exercise did make a clear profit of nearly £1,500 for Grahame-White. It also showed the continuing unreliability and safety hazards of flying when one of the pilots crash-landed and broke both his legs.

Only one year earlier another aviation pioneer, Charles Rolls, had been the first Briton to be killed in a flying accident when the tail of his Wright Flyer broke off during a flying display near Bournemouth. A month before his death Rolls had become the first man to make a non-stop double crossing of the English Channel by plane, taking 95 minutes – faster than Blériot on his one-way trip.[13]

In 1911 there was nothing in Britain that could be described as an airline service of any kind. The only contender in Europe was the use of rigid airships pioneered by the German Count Ferdinand von Zeppelin (1838–1917), who operated special inter-city flights and sightseeing tours for over 30,000 passengers between 1910 and 1914. It was not a regular air service, but the impressive development of Zeppelin airships in Germany created an enthusiasm and popular support for aviation there that was unmatched in Britain.

The modernity and growing speed of the aeroplane was also an inspiration to artists, particularly the Italian group who styled themselves the Futurists. They were attracted to the dynamism of aircraft and other fast-moving machines, though in the early years of aviation very few artists found effective ways to capture an impression of speed in oils or other media. Most early aviation posters are curiously static

12 Flying at Hendon
Designer: Tony Sarg
Underground poster, 1913

13 **Flying at Hendon,**
Go by Underground
Designer: Tony Sarg
Underground poster, 1914

14 **Aero Exhibition Olympia**
Unknown designer
Underground poster, 1913

and even the elaborate Schneider Trophy, offered in 1911 by a wealthy French industrialist as the prize in an annual international race for fast seaplanes, is an elaborate art nouveau confection that has no real hint of speed or movement about it.[14] More appropriate representations of flight in art and design would come with the development of art deco, modernism and streamlining from the late 1920s, particularly in the United States.[15]

The world's first airline is considered to be the St Petersburg–Tampa Airboat line established in Florida by Percy Fansler. It began operating on 1 January 1914, carrying a single passenger at a time across Tampa Bay in a flying boat, a fast and direct alternative to the circuitous land route by rail. The service closed after just three months, confirming that even in the United States there was no market as yet for an expensive and exclusive personal service that was more akin to an aerial taxi than a passenger route.

By coincidence, the potential for running a regular service with a large aircraft able to carry up to 16 passengers, then an unprecedented capacity, was shown in the Russian city of St Petersburg only a few months later. On 30 June 1914, Igor Sikorsky,[16] with a crew of three, took off on an epic flight in his new, giant, four-engine transport aircraft from the Russian imperial capital. With just one stop on the way he reached Kiev, 9,300 miles (15,000 km) due south of St Petersburg, on 12 July.

Aviation historians credit Sikorsky with the design, development and demonstration of the world's first practical airliner and transport plane. But at the time his achievement was immediately overtaken by international events. Within days of his touchdown in Kiev, virtually the whole of Europe, including Russia, was embroiled in the First World War.[17]

War and Peace

The outbreak of war in August 1914 closed down all plans for commercial aviation development in Europe before any service had started, and a new period of rapid technological advance in aviation was driven by military requirements. One of the major international aeronautical events planned for September 1914 was a grand flying festival to celebrate the opening of the port of Brussels. A surviving copy of a striking advertising poster produced by the Aero Club of Belgium earlier in the year depicts four '*hydroaéroplanes*' landing on the waterfront in peaceful competition. The event, needless to say, was cancelled and by September most of Belgium had been occupied by invading German forces heading for France. When their advance was halted by French and British forces four years of dug-in stalemate and trench warfare all along the Western Front ensued.[18]

While technical innovation and mass production methods were concentrated on military aircraft development for the duration of the war, there were farsighted individuals who foresaw a new era of civil aviation in peacetime. In the United Kingdom one of the most articulate of these was the industrialist

George Holt Thomas (1869–1929), who made the first practical move towards this by registering the Aircraft Transport & Travel (AT&T) company as early as 1916.

AT&T was a subsidiary of Holt Thomas' Aircraft Manufacturing Company, known as Airco, which had grown rapidly in wartime to become the largest aircraft production enterprise in the world. Holt Thomas, whose wealth came originally from the London publishing empire inherited from his father, had become interested in aviation in 1909. He started building under licence the simple but easy to fly bi-planes designed by the French Farman brothers, and supplying them to the British Army. When war came Holt Thomas took on the most talented British aircraft designer of the day, Geoffrey de Havilland (1882–1965), and his creations went into massive production for military use.

In a lecture to the Royal Aeronautical Society in 1917, Holt Thomas presented his ideas on the future of commercial flying. With the help of his friend Lord Montagu of Beaulieu, an influential supporter of aviation, he persuaded David Lloyd George, leader of the wartime coalition government, to

15 Inauguration of the Port of Brussels, Circuit of Three Rivers
Designer: Louis-Marie Lemaire
Aero Club of Belgium
poster, 1914

There were international air shows and competitions all over Europe from around 1910. This beautifully produced poster advertised seaplane races in Brussels to celebrate the opening of a new inland port facility on the Rhine planned for September 1914. The event was cancelled with the outbreak of war one month earlier and the rapid invasion of Belgium by the German Army.

set up a parliamentary Civil Aerial Transport Committee. This was chaired by aviation enthusiast Lord Northcliffe and reported back in February 1918, nine months before the war ended.

Northcliffe's committee strongly recommended state support for post-war air transport services and the creation of Empire air routes across the world as a priority for peacetime. However, this was effectively shelved by the government by the time the post-war world was being hammered out at Versailles just over a year later.

A special 'Golden Peace' issue of Northcliffe's *Daily Mail*, published in June 1919 as the terms of the peace treaty were announced, pushed hard for Britain to use this opportunity to promote its civil aviation to a wider audience than politicians: 'The War has bequeathed to us as a nation a great heritage in the air. Our pilots are the best, our designs the most efficient, and our industry the greatest in the world. Supremacy in the air is ours for the making.' The writer was Major-General Sir Sefton Brancker (1877–1930), Britain's former Comptroller General of Equipment during the war, who now joined Holt Thomas at AT&T to develop commercial aviation in peacetime.

Soon afterwards Holt Thomas committed his visionary ideas to print in a remarkably farsighted book called *Aerial Transport*, published in 1920 with an introduction by Northcliffe. 'London to New York will certainly become a commercial proposition,' he wrote, 'but only in stages; probably, as far as possible by long distance machines and the practical flying boat.'

Even as Holt Thomas was writing, the technical feasibility of transatlantic flight was demonstrated by two RAF pilots, John Alcock and Arthur Whitten Brown, in their epic 1,890 mile (3,040 km), 16-hour journey from Newfoundland to Ireland in June 1919, flying in a converted Vickers

16 Statue of John Alcock and Arthur Whitten Brown, Heathrow

This memorial to the two RAF pilots who were the first to fly the North Atlantic from Newfoundland to Ireland in 1919 was unveiled at London Heathrow in 1954.

Vimy bomber. It was an extremely hazardous non-stop flight in appalling weather conditions, which nearly ended in disaster several times owing to engine trouble, fog, snow and ice. They only just made it, crash-landing in a bog near Clifton, on the coast of County Galway, where the locals laughed in disbelief when first told by the pair that they had flown the Atlantic. Both men were feted as heroes and knighted by the King at Windsor Castle. They also became the winners of yet another aviation prize originally put up by the *Daily Mail* in 1913 but previously uncontested because of the war.

Tragically, Alcock was killed in an air crash only six months later, trying to land in thick fog while delivering a new Vickers plane to the first post-war

17 Preparing for the first commercial flight from London to Paris at Hounslow Heath, 25 August 1919. The plane is a DH.4A operated by Aircraft Transport & Travel, a company that was established by Holt Thomas during the First World War but was unable to start scheduled services until after the peace treaty had been signed in July 1919.

Aero Exhibition in Paris. Alcock's death confirmed once again the dangers of flying and the high level of risk that so many young aviators were willing to take. His grief-stricken co-pilot and engineer, Brown, never flew again, but Alcock's elder brother, who had been a fellow pilot in the Royal Flying Corps, later became a captain with Imperial Airways and flew on many of the long-distance Empire routes. The dream of transatlantic passenger air travel was to be achieved only after another 20 years, before being postponed as a regular service by the outbreak of another war.[19]

The more immediate problem that arose in 1919–20, and was inevitably more pressing for aviation entrepreneurs than safety, was how to make commercial flying profitable. Ignoring the advice of Northcliffe's committee, the government made civil flying legal again after the peace agreement but left private enterprise to get on with it. Holt Thomas' AT&T and the company of rival aircraft builder, Frederick Handley Page (1885–1962), started running separate scheduled air services from Hounslow and Cricklewood in London to Paris and Brussels in 1919.

Even those politicians keen for British civil aviation to succeed failed to see the need for any financial assistance from government to get it underway on a sound basis. In 1920 Winston Churchill, briefly responsible for air policy as Secretary of State for War and Air, remarked

18 A Daily Air Parcel Post to Paris & Brussels
Unknown designer
Instone Airline advertising card, c.1922

This display card was hung up in Post Offices. Instone was one of the four small independent airlines that were merged to form Imperial Airways in 1924.

19 Parcel Post Service to Paris, Send Parcels by Air
Unknown designer
Post Office display card, c.1923

A display card probably produced by the Post Office as no specific airline is mentioned. The aircraft shown is a converted First World War bomber.

characteristically in the House of Commons that 'Civil aviation must fly by itself; the Government cannot possibly hold it up in the air.'[20]

This was easier said than done, even for experienced businessmen like Holt Thomas and Handley Page, who had both profited handsomely from government contracts during the war. Their new civil aviation companies used converted military aircraft and promised rapid, comfortable, passenger journeys by air, but soon found they were making heavy financial losses. For prospective travellers even a trip across the Channel by air looked pricey and a little risky.

The Paris route attracted competition from two other British companies, but more significantly from two subsidised French airlines who effectively forced them out of business. Handley Page could not run the Paris service at a fare below ten guineas (£10.50) but the French government-backed continental airlines were charging only six guineas (£6.30). None of the British airlines could even fill the limited capacity of their planes. By February 1921 all the British companies had suspended

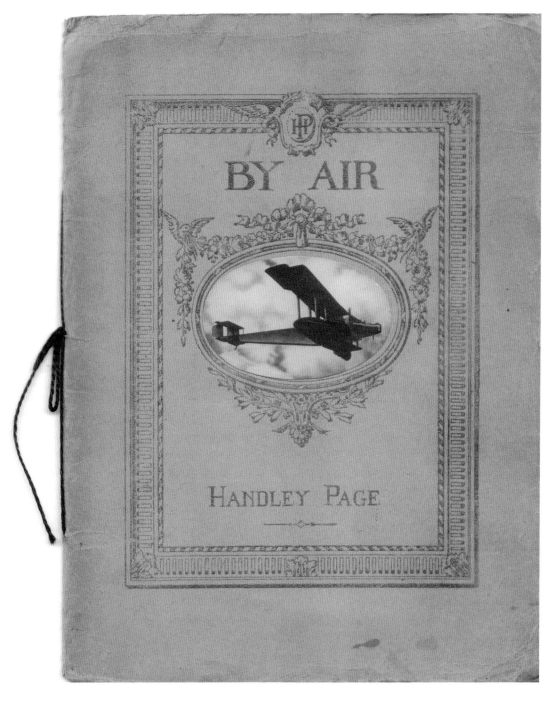

This promotional brochure contains a hair-raising account of a flight from London to Paris, which seems more likely to have frightened off rather than encouraged prospective passengers. Early flying was not for the faint-hearted. Handley Page had built hundreds of large 0/400 bombers during the First World War, most of which were now redundant. A few were converted to provide early civilian passenger transport, for which they were not really suitable.

services and civil aviation in Britain had effectively collapsed after just 18 months of operation.

The government came to the rescue by offering temporary subsidies to individual British airlines operating on the main London–Paris route. Subsidised services were also introduced on other European routes from London to Amsterdam, Brussels and beyond, and there were internal flights from London to Manchester and from Southampton to the Channel Islands. By 1923 the principal domestic services were all being run by four small companies.[21] Passenger traffic to the Continent doubled in just two years, but none of the companies was making a profit and their prospects did not look good.

The pioneer British airlines were caught in a vicious circle. Their ex-military aircraft were inefficient and mostly unsuitable for running commercial services. The planes were under-powered, had low capacity and high operating and maintenance costs. Freight and mail services, which the companies had hoped would provide the mainstay of their new business, failed to develop. Passenger traffic, which they initially expected to be of secondary importance, was soon providing most of their income, but it was highly seasonal. The unreliability of services, especially in bad weather and in winter, was a constant problem. Even when fares were reduced on the London–Paris run a return air fare was more than twice the cost of a first-class ticket by rail and ship.[22]

21 Shell Aviation Spirit
Unknown designer
Shell poster, 1921

22 Waddon Aerodrome, Change Cars at West Croydon
Designer: Aldo Cosomati
Underground poster, 1921

This poster was issued by the Underground Group to promote excursion trips to the aerodrome by the company's tramcars (the 'cars' of the title). Waddon had been renamed Croydon aerodrome a few months before this poster was produced but clearly not in time to alter the printing.

The Birth of Imperial

The obvious solution, which Holt Thomas and others had advocated, was the creation of a single large airline company with government backing. Having just reduced the enormous number of private railway companies in Britain to the 'big four',[23] the government now gave proper attention to how the new airline industry should be organised and run. Another government committee, this one under Lord Hambling, concluded in 1923 that the single company route was indeed the best way forward, and this time the government acted on its advice.

On 31 March 1924 the government's 'chosen instrument', Imperial Airways, was created with a capital of £1 million, having bought out the four small, independent airline companies. Sir Eric Geddes (1875–1937), a former railway manager who had served in Lloyd George's wartime administration and become the first Minister of Transport in 1919, was made Imperial's first chairman. The new managing director was former motor engineer Frank Searle,[24] who joined from Daimler Air Hire. George Woods Humphery,[25] also from Daimler and previously with Handley

Page, became general manager. Between them, the new Imperial team appeared to have a good record of engineering and management experience, but they were plunged into immediate conflict with their pilots, who went on strike in a dispute over their contracts.

An Air Superintendent, Herbert Brackley (1894–1948), was appointed to represent the pilots' interests, and passenger services only began after three weeks of negotiation brought about an agreement. Brackley's role soon expanded into taking the lead in route development and planning, which according to Captain G.J. Powell, one of the senior company pilots, was 'brilliantly done'. His position as an intermediary between staff and management was more uncomfortable and problematic. In Powell's view, 'Brackley was miscast, because he lacked the hard edge and short fuse that would have stopped some of our prima donnas, and believe me we had plenty of them.'[26]

Geddes had a reputation for impatience and was said to regard his pilots as no different to the engine drivers who had worked for him when he ran the North Eastern Railway. Staff relations

LONDON 2026 A.D.—THIS IS ALL IN THE AIR

TO·DAY — THE SOLID COMFORT OF THE UNDERGROUND

24 Signed souvenir postcards of Imperial Airways pilots, c.1927

Captain Horsey (right) is posing in front of a seaplane used on the Channel Islands service from Southampton.

at Imperial were often particularly difficult between the management and the operational side, and even within the managerial group there were serious divisions early on. Searle, the managing director, left in April 1925 after only a year in post, and Woods Humphery took over. He stayed in post until 1938 but often faced criticism and disputes both internally and from outside the company.

Imperial was particularly slow at getting a grip on public relations, and this is where some advice on transforming potential difficulties into good publicity in the early days might have helped. The company did not have an equivalent talent to Frank Pick, who had risen to become assistant managing director of the London Underground in the 1920s. Pick was already demonstrating better than anyone how an organisation with a mediocre reputation could be transformed through a culture of good design management and a firm application of 'fitness for purpose' principles in every area.

The Underground was a much larger organisation than Imperial Airways at this time, but was a model of progressive management with a very positive public image reinforced by Pick's popular poster programme, which turned every station platform into a gallery of modern art and design. In contrast, aviation poster design did not become a significant feature of British airline publicity until the 1930s.

Imperial Airways was not viewed in the same positive light as the Underground by the public, politicians or the fledgling aviation industry. It faced a lot of adverse comment at its poor performance in the early days on everything from the design of its planes to the unreliability of its services. In particular, it did not look good when compared with its foreign competitors. At the end of 1926, when the company proudly announced that it had carried 16,652 passengers in and out of England, a Member of Parliament asked in the House of Commons how this figure compared with German airline traffic. He was told that the information was not available. The editor of the *Aeroplane* magazine, the leading specialist weekly on aviation matters, commented sarcastically that, 'comparing Imperial Airways traffic with German traffic is like comparing traffic out of Penzance railway station with that of Manchester'.[27] It was well known that Deutsche Luft Hansa (as Lufthansa was then known), which had just been put together as a single airline company for Germany, was already the biggest air-traffic combine in the world.

This was particularly galling for the British, who had won the war less than a decade earlier but were already losing out to foreign competitors on a number of airline routes into Europe. Imperial soon abandoned its Amsterdam service to KLM, the Dutch national airline, and left all Berlin services to Luft Hansa. By 1928 a London newspaper was reporting that Germany had 160 airliners flying more than 64,300 km (40,000 miles) each day and carrying nearly 20,000 passengers a month.[28]

Imperial's apparent lack of drive and its retreat from these markets did not go down well. Although it was in theory an independent company, Imperial had been effectively granted a monopoly of airline operation in Britain by the government. No other company would be offered state aid for a period of ten years and if a rival business were to be set up, it was almost bound to fail. Imperial would get an annual subsidy of up to £1 million from the government over those ten years. This was supposed to be reduced over time as traffic developed and (it was hoped) Imperial became a self-supporting business making fewer demands on the taxpayer.

In practice the company seemed unable to grow the business and the annual subsidy increased every year. At the same time shareholders were guaranteed a dividend even if the company failed to make a profit. Under the terms of its original government agreement, Imperial undertook to fly an average of one million miles per year and to develop a range of new, efficient and commercially desirable services. All equipment used by the company, both aircraft and engines, had to be British-made and all aircraft had to be equipped with apparatus for safe and proper navigation. Progress in these areas was patchy and Imperial's procurement procedures with aircraft designers and manufacturers were not always robust, but the company did recognise early on that its greatest publicity assets were men, not machines. Early passengers were keenly aware that their safety was almost entirely in the hands of their pilots, and these men soon acquired both heroic and pin-up status. Imperial even started issuing signed official postcards of their top pilots, posing beside their aircraft in full flying gear like film stars.

It was already clear to the authorities, not just in Britain but throughout Europe, that only international air services stood any chance of commercial success. For Britain in particular, restricting operations to Europe made no sense and Imperial set its sights further afield. As the chairman, Sir Eric Geddes, put it at the first annual general meeting in 1925:

It is axiomatic in civil aviation that the greater the distance the greater is the advantage of flying that distance, and your company must stretch forth its services so as to reap that advantage over older and slower methods of transport. Confined to short routes such as London–Paris and London–Berlin, the progress of commercial aviation must be slow … the very name of your company implies that we should not be justified in confining operations to short European routes (hear, hear!).[29]

Linking the Empire

At this stage the company still had a long way to go. The name of the national flag-carrier became increasingly appropriate and significant because the network that Imperial Airways created in its 15-year existence was closely linked to the British Empire, and to a particular view of the Empire's role and purpose that developed in the inter-war years. This in turn was reflected in both the operation and image of the airline in a period when advertising, publicity and design were becoming ever more significant aspects of everyday life.

The years after the Great War were turbulent times both politically and economically. Pre-war notions of rapid and continuous change driven by technological improvement, which could bring about better living standards, no longer seemed certain or predictable. The war had shown how technical innovations like the aeroplane could be applied as effectively to destructive military purposes as to more obvious areas of social progress. Art and design, influenced by new developments like moving pictures in the cinema, followed by radio and sound film, were now applied with growing sophistication to advertising and propaganda in the consumer societies of Europe and the United States.

Many people in Britain saw the Empire dominions as having an even more critical and supportive role for the home country in the twentieth century than they had played in the Victorian period. Civil aviation, with its capacity to shrink the world, save time and bind the Empire together, could become an essential new global tie for British society.[30] There was certainly a wish for Imperial Airways to play a major role in European aviation but, as the name implies, the real goal of the airline from the start was to build an Empire network and that was clearly going to take time. It would also mean that the stylish poster and publicity campaigns for which Imperial became well known in the 1930s followed on from, and were strongly influenced by, other large, image-conscious organisations of the period.

Amongst transport companies the Underground group already led the publicity field in the early 1920s, followed by the mainline railways, the major shipping lines and other big companies linked to transport such as Shell. A new government agency, the Empire Marketing Board, ran a persuasive visual

25 Comfort Routes
Unknown designer
Imperial Airways poster, c.1930

A winged armchair, moderne typography and just a hint of art-deco styling.

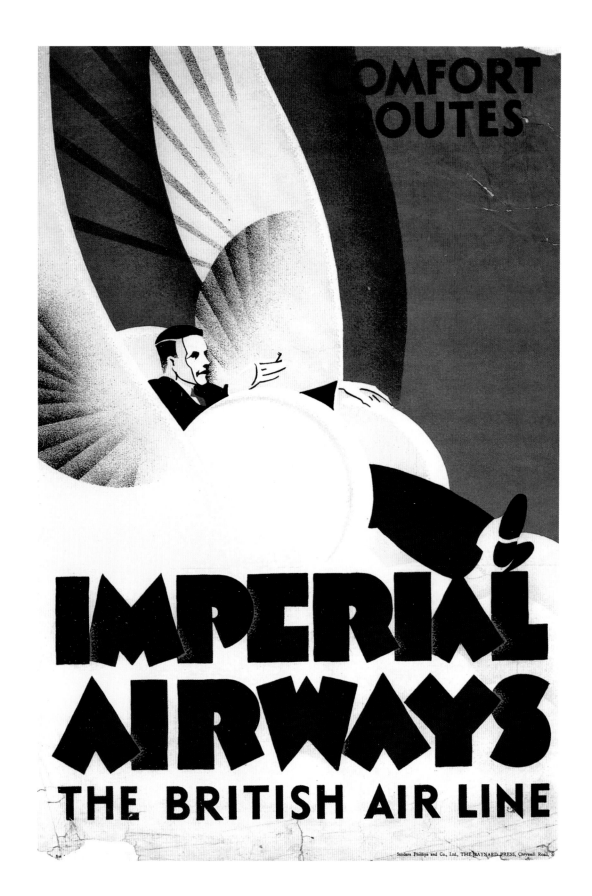

IMPERIAL AIRWAYS

have pleasure in announcing

the FIRST
AIR PLEASURE CRUISE

THIS is the first air pleasure Cruise in the world. It departs on January 31 and returns on March 5, 1928. February is usually the worst month of the year. This Cruise enables you to exchange the foggy, leaden skies of February for the sunny, bright, joyous climes of Southern France, Spain, Northern Africa, and Italy. It has been designed to obviate any bother to passengers, and to ensure *de luxe* travel and accommodation throughout the Cruise —which lasts thirty-five days.

Full particulars of the Cruise can be obtained from any Travel Agency, or from Imperial Airways, Ltd., Airways House, Charles Street, Lower Regent Street, London, S.W.1.

propaganda campaign, mainly through posters, between 1926 and 1933.[31] The British Broadcasting Corporation, founded as a private company in 1922 but turned into a public corporation only five years later, was highly influential through the new medium of radio, which included an Empire service from 1932. Even the traditionally staid General Post Office adopted a public relations strategy in the early 1930s, commissioning posters and surprisingly innovative documentary films. Some of these organisations determined their own in-house approach to publicity and branding while others hired newly booming advertising agencies and professional designers to shape their public image.

IMPERIAL AIRWAYS USE
THROUGHOUT EUROPE

SHELL PETROL EXCLUSIVELY

For Imperial Airways it was a combination of the two, but its approach was to plan and develop the physical building blocks of a national airline before it spent time and money promoting it. Concentrating on the technical practicalities of creating an increasingly reliable, engineering-led service in the 1920s made it possible to promote the Imperial brand with confidence and creativity in the 1930s.

In the early years the company was slow on the uptake. Within a limited budget, allocating staff or financial resources to either publicity or public relations was considered an unnecessary luxury for Imperial. Charles Higham (1876–1938) provided consultancy services to the company through his agency, but his old-fashioned approach to advertising, which relied on wordy testimonials and purple prose in press advertisements, would have been inappropriate to promoting a new

airline. Visual promotion through posters or well-illustrated magazine advertising was not his style, and Imperial did not appear at all in the early volumes of *Commercial Art* magazine, which from 1922 established itself as the arbiter of quality in the new world of publicity design.

It would be wrong to suggest that Imperial developed in the 1920s along a smooth, pre-determined flight path. Even after the pilots' dispute had been settled, disagreements within the management led, as already mentioned, to the departure of Searle, the original managing director, at the end of his first year in post. Woods Humphery took over as managing director in 1925 and led the company until the late 1930s, but not without criticism. He had a confident but somewhat arrogant approach, which would eventually be his undoing in 1938 when he was effectively dismissed by an even more autocratic new company chairman.[32]

27 Imperial Airways use Shell Petrol Exclusively
Designer: Dacres Adams
Shell poster, 1929

One of Shell's striking 'lorry bill' posters which were displayed on the sides of the company's delivery trucks. This shows a three-engine Argosy airliner on the concrete apron at Croydon in front of the control tower, which opened in 1928. There were no runways at Croydon and both take-off and landing were on grass.

28 Go There by Air Taxi
Unknown designer
Imperial Airways poster, c.1930

Imperial offered air-taxi services using small light aircraft within Britain and Europe.

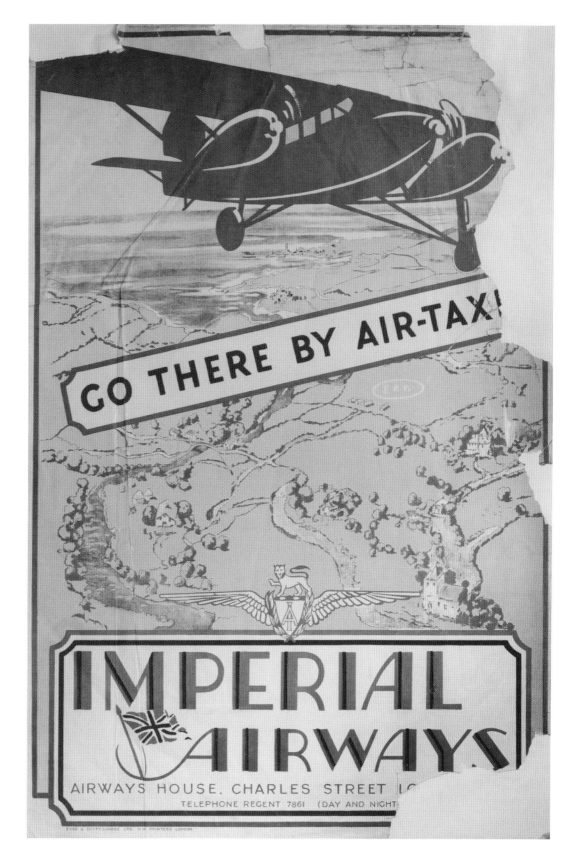

Aspiring to the Name

When Imperial Airways was established as the national carrier, it owned a motley fleet of just 15 assorted aircraft inherited from the four previous private operators. There were six different types, while two of the aircraft were seaplanes and two others could not be flown. Two further aircraft had crashed and been scrapped before the end of the year and two more were dismantled as unusable. Providing long-distance air travel at this stage was out of the question.

Imperial started from such a low base in 1924 that over-promotion of the product before it could be delivered would have been a serious mistake. In 1924–5, at the British Empire Exhibition at Wembley, a huge, popular celebration of the culture and products of Empire, there was no premature attempt to advertise the aspirations of Imperial Airways before the prospective Empire routes had even been surveyed.

At a special Imperial Congress held at the Wembley exhibition, Sir Sefton Brancker, Director of Civil Aviation since 1922, gave a revealing speech on 'Imperial Communications'. While recognising the enormous potential in aviation development,

he was short on government policy and cagey on commitment. Reading between the lines, it is obvious that the government had not yet decided on a clear course of action. He talked of commercial airship development on long-distance routes linking the Empire, but revealed that so far the government had simply commissioned two large rival airships, one from the state and one from private enterprise, for comparative trials. In a very modern way, the politicians were clearly hedging their bets, but Brancker confidently predicted a bi-weekly airship service for passengers and mail to India and Australia before long.[33]

Brancker also talked of the development expectations from Imperial Airways of European services, but looked ahead to long-distance Empire routes in the near future as the real way forward. From its tiny start-up fleet of aircraft, Imperial should have grown over ten years:

to own at least 100 heavy machines carrying 30 or 40 passengers ... I doubt if the speed of ordinary passenger-carrying aircraft will be much above 100 mph even 10 years hence,

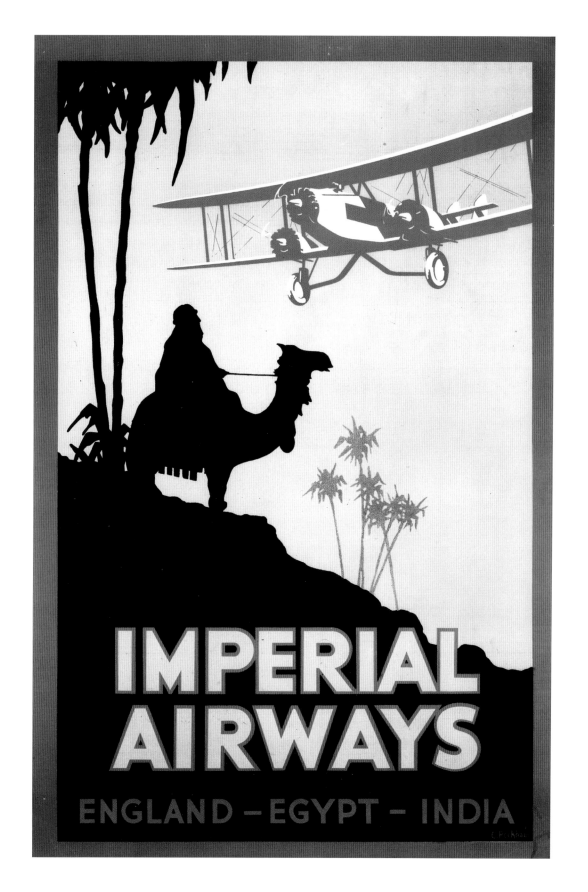

IMPERIAL
AIRWAYS

ENGLAND — EGYPT — INDIA

THE INDIAN COURTYARD.

ERNEST COFFIN

but I anticipate that by that time the air mail will be firmly established in Europe, and that aircraft travelling at 140 mph and carrying letters only will be leaving England along at least four different important mail routes.

Brancker himself was another apostle of the air, whatever the doubts of his fellow representatives of government:

The rich men of the world seem slow to realise the great possibilities of this form of travel; it does seem ridiculous that this means of visiting every business centre in Europe at short notice and with the utmost rapidity is not far more used than it actually is.

It is only necessary to obtain real solid support for these enterprises from the public, and the money would be found; but it is that universal public support which is so difficult to develop. The public are learning, however, and very clear demands for the development

30 East meets West
Designer: Ernest Coffin

A postcard view of the Indian Courtyard at the British Empire Exhibition, Wembley, 1924. In Imperial Airways' first year of operation the prospect of being able to fly to far flung empire destinations still looked like a distant dream.

31 Alan Cobham (left) and Director of Civil Aviation Sir Sefton Brancker preparing for their route survey flight to India, 1924.

of air transport are beginning to take form. Air transport is coming as a great boon to the British Empire ...(we must) waste no time. The rapidity and efficiency of our imperial communications may well be the measure of our success – or our failure – to hold our empire together in the future.[34]

While the press and the public were invariably interested in new speed or endurance records by aviators, Imperial Airways now had to be more concerned with the preparation of airfields and water landings, climate and meteorological forecasts, installations and personnel requirements along thousands of miles of future airline routes through Asia and Africa.

Alan Cobham (1894–1973), a member of the Royal Flying Corps during the war and later a test pilot for the de Havilland Aircraft Company, became famous for his long-distance aerial survey work for Imperial in the 1920s. In November 1924, soon after Brancker's address at Wembley, Cobham

1926

set out on his first 18,000 mile (29,000 km) aerial survey trip to India, accompanied by engineer Alan Elliott. Amazingly enough, Sir Sefton Brancker actually travelled with them in the cramped little bi-plane, which showed extraordinary dedication for a politician.

In 1925–6 Cobham made another memorable survey flight through Africa, mapping out a potential Imperial Airways route to Cape Town. This time he took a skilled Gaumont film cameraman with him, who took some of the first aerial footage of locations from Cairo to the Cape. Only three months after his return to London, Cobham set off on a third epic return journey to Australia. He made a spectacular landing on the River Thames outside the Houses of Parliament on 1 October 1926 after 28,000 miles (45,000 km) of flying, and was greeted by a large and excited crowd of spectators. 'The Nation Welcomes Cobham Home' was the front page headline of the *Daily Graphic* next morning, over photographs of his dramatic landing. His aquatic arrival was appropriate as the use of specially designed flying boats rather than adapted landplanes like his own would become a key part of the strategy for developing services on sections of the Empire routes

Cobham had surveyed, where land airports were difficult and/or expensive to establish.

Alan Cobham was knighted for his achievement, his trusty, open cockpit, de Havilland DH.50 was put on display in Selfridges department store (just as Blériot's Channel-crossing monoplane had been in 1909) and the films taken on his journeys were shown in cinemas all over the country. Cobham became the most celebrated British airman of the day, devoted to the notion of making the country 'air-minded' as he liked to put it, and as skilled at publicity as he was at flying. His own entertaining account of the flight to Australia, published soon after the trip, ends with his reception on the terrace of the House of Commons, having come straight up the Palace Landing Stairs from the river: 'At the close of that tremendous day I think I went to bed convinced that at last the public realised the importance of aviation to every Briton, and – what is more – I felt that its imagination was aroused in support of this good cause. I hope I was right.'[35]

Cobham's aircraft on all three of his long-distance survey trips was a single engine DH.50[36] with room for the pilot and two passengers. At the end of 1926, Imperial took delivery of new tri-motor DH.66 Hercules airliners, specially built by de Havilland for use on its first Middle East services. From January 1927 Imperial took over the Desert Air Mail service from Cairo to Basra, pioneered in 1921 by the RAF as a transport service across the Arabian Desert. As well as carrying the post, the Hercules airliners could now carry up to seven passengers. The pilot was still in an open cockpit (as all of them preferred to be at this time) while his passengers sat in an enclosed cabin, from which it was possible to open the windows and lean out. It was not exactly luxury travel, but this marked the first crucial stage of the planned Empire air routes beyond Europe. Others were soon to follow.

32 Alan Cobham landing on the River Thames outside the Houses of Parliament on his return from surveying an Imperial route to Australia. Part of the large crowd there to greet him can be seen gathered on Westminster Bridge, 1 October 1926.

33 An Imperial Airways African services brochure that has been stamped and sent through the Air Mail system, 1931. Unknown designer.

IMPERIAL AIRWAYS

THE BRITISH AIR LINE

Passenger, Freight and Air Mail Services
from LONDON to

FRANCE
GERMANY
SWITZERLAND
BELGIUM

With connections to all parts of Europe

EGYPT
PALESTINE
IRAQ
PERSIA
INDIA
EGYPTIAN SUDAN
MONGALLA
UGANDA
KENYA
TANGANYIKA
&c.   &c.

Full particulars from any of the Company's
Stations or from :—

SENDER :-

H.C. Myers Esq., A.I.D.
British Civil Aviation Directora
Heliopolis Aerodrome,
Heliopolis,
Cairo.
Egypt.

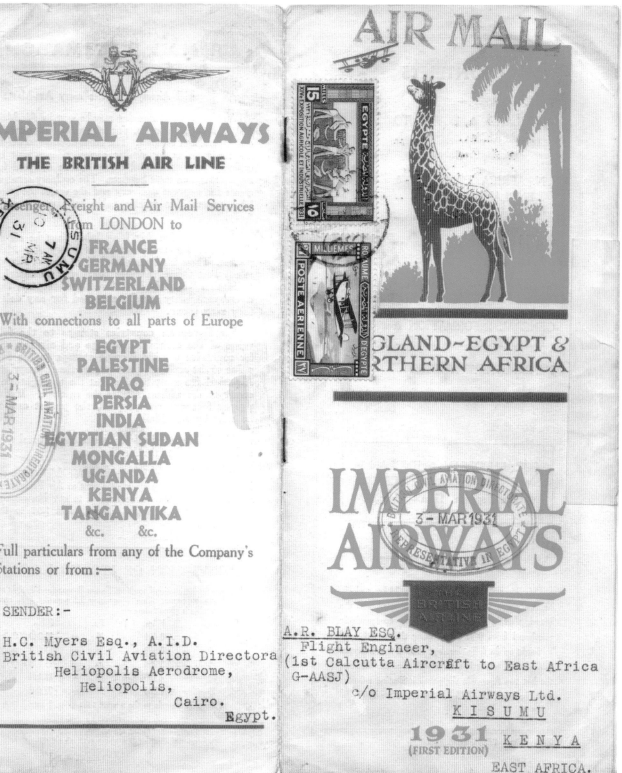

AIR MAIL

ENGLAND~EGYPT &
NORTHERN AFRICA

IMPERIAL AIRWAYS
THE BRITISH AIR LINE

A.R. BLAY ESQ.
Flight Engineer,
(1st Calcutta Aircraft to East Africa
G-AASJ)
c/o Imperial Airways Ltd.
KISUMU
1931   KENYA
(FIRST EDITION)

EAST AFRICA.

Croydon and the Wider World

While the long-distance Empire services were progressively introduced from the late 1920s, starting with the Desert Air Mail, Imperial at last upgraded its European air routes with new purpose-built airliners. The 18-seat Armstrong Whitworth Argosy, first introduced on the London–Paris service in 1926, was arguably the first ever luxury air service. This had become the busiest air route in the world and it was important for Imperial to compete more effectively with its main French rival, Air Union.

On 1 May 1927 Imperial introduced its 'Silver Wing' full catering service. The Argosy had spacious passenger cabins and for £1 extra passengers got a meal and drinks service from a uniformed steward on their 2 hour 30 minute journey from Croydon to Paris. Air Union responded with the 'Golden Ray' catering service but Imperial countered with a choice of fast first-class or slower but cheaper second-class services using older planes.

Comfort and safety, rather than speed, became the characteristic superior features on which Imperial sold its European services. The Argosy scored highly on both counts but it was not fast, with a top speed of only 90 mph (145 km/h). In a staged race in 1928 against the London & North Eastern Railway's crack London–Edinburgh express, the *Flying Scotsman*, which had just become non-stop on its 393-mile (632 km) journey, an Imperial airliner only just beat the train by 15 minutes. This performance did not suggest that the railways needed to worry about potential competition from airlines on domestic routes, but a year later the four mainline railway companies did secure powers to run their own air services. They did not start planning to actually do this until the early 1930s when some motor-coach companies began to move into the domestic airline market.[37]

Imperial's home base was at Croydon, 10 miles (16 km) south of London. The former military airfield at Beddington and the National Aircraft Factory site at nearby Waddon were combined in 1920 to create Croydon Aerodrome, the official customs airport for London. Three of the pioneer airlines moved in and the site gradually expanded with a ramshackle collection of huts and hangars. It looked like a shanty town when Imperial took over in 1924, but three years later purpose-built facilities were put up on the opposite side of the site.[38]

34 Imperial Airways
Designer: Harold McCready
Imperial Airways poster, c.1930

The incongruously bright Mediterranean colours make this scene at Croydon look like a desert aerodrome in North Africa.

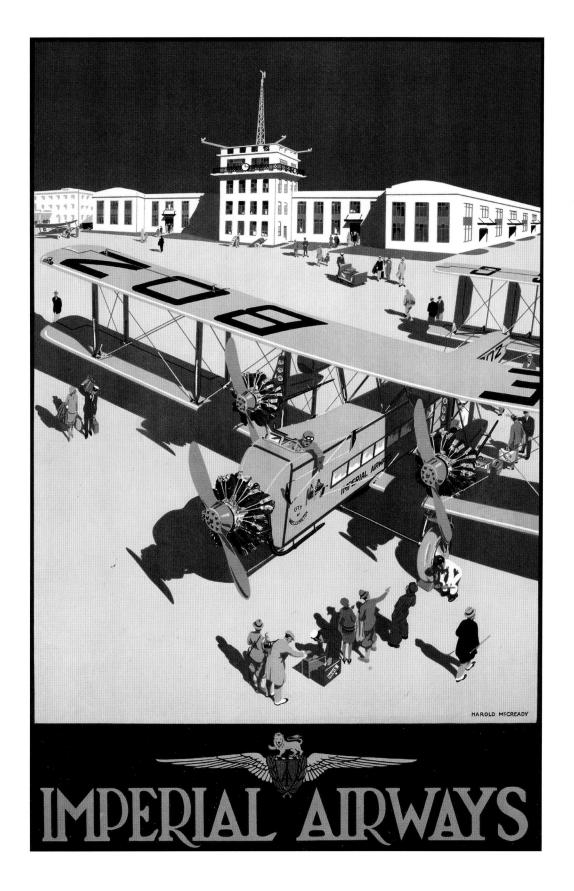

HAROLD McCREADY

IMPERIAL AIRWAYS

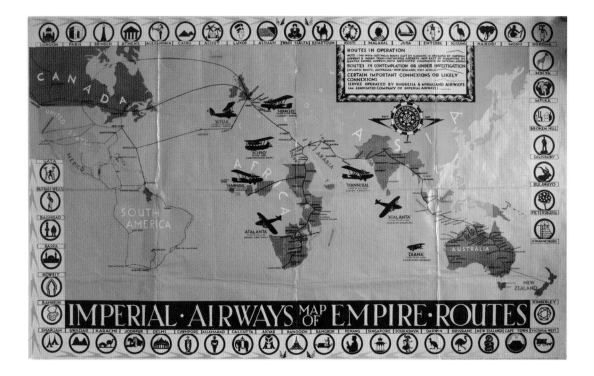

When American aviator Charles Lindbergh (1902–74) flew in to Croydon on 29 May 1927 after completing the first solo Atlantic crossing, he was greeted by more than 200,000 people. According to the airport's historians, 'on this day Croydon saw probably the largest crowds to assemble at any airport to meet an incoming flight; certainly until the return of the Beatles to Heathrow from the USA in 1964'. A press report described police and officials as 'powerless to control the stampede'. As for the crowd, a British journalist for the *Aeroplane* magazine wrote 'They behaved just like a lot of foreigners.'[39]

Almost exactly a year after Lindbergh's chaotic reception, the official opening of the new airport was performed by Lady Mary Hoare, wife of Sir Samuel, the Air Minister. 'Among the large assembly that witnessed the ceremony were many well known airmen,' reported *The Times*. 'The transformation of the Croydon Aerodrome has already been appreciated by passengers to and from the Continent. In contrast to the unsatisfactory conditions which have prevailed since civil aviation began in 1919, they now find a convenient landing stage, pleasant waiting rooms, more light and warmth, and even an hotel.'[40]

An early travel guide claimed that Croydon demonstrated that 'Civil Aviation in England has been established on a sound basis … it is a reality and not a toy played with by enthusiasts'.[41] This was partly true, but far more people visited Croydon simply to watch the planes rather than travel on a scheduled flight. As even a cross-Channel trip to Paris was still expensive the only experience of flight that was more widely accessible was a short joyride round the airfield. It was much the same at Hendon Aerodrome, where in the post-war period the RAF was offering an annual 'aerial pageant' from 1920. Every year more than 60,000 visitors to the pageant would watch elaborate demonstrations of aerial combat, sky writing, parachuting and bombing raids on 'native villages' as well as getting the chance to 'loop the loop' themselves as a passenger. These shows became even more popular when the Hampstead Tube was extended to Edgware in 1924 and a station was opened at Colindale, close to the airfield.

For most people the vicarious thrill of seeing a plane land or take off was quite sufficient, and both commercial pilots and lone aviators achieved the star status of Hollywood idols. Lindbergh had been received with acclaim but there was almost

35 Imperial Airways Map of Empire Routes
Unknown designer
Imperial Airways poster, *c*.1935

JUNE 27th (Saturday)   TRAVEL [UNDERGROUND]
Book to COLINDALE (adjoins Aerodrome)or HENDON
                STATIONS

36 RAF Display
Designer: Charles E. Turner
Underground poster, 1925

A small panel poster designed for display inside Underground carriages to advertise the annual RAF pageant. Aerial advertising with sign-writing was a short-lived fad in the inter-war years.

more excitement about the return of Amy Johnson (1903–41) three years after Lindbergh's flight.[42]

Johnson had set off from Croydon in May 1930 on her solo flight to Australia in her second-hand DH.60 Gipsy Moth *Jason* virtually without ceremony. By the time she arrived in Darwin nearly one month later, the press had made her famous internationally as 'The Lone Girl Flyer', 'The Empire's Wonderful Woman' and 'Aeroplane Girl'. Her return journey was largely by sea and Imperial Airways airliner, but she did fly into Croydon on the final leg on 4 August 1930, when large crowds were there to cheer her in. 'Amy Swoops to Croydon. Aerodrome Magnet for Young and Old. Air Queen's Homecoming'[43] ran the headline in the local paper, reflecting national rather than purely local excitement.

Amy Johnson epitomised the extraordinary peak of popular interest in aviation in Britain at this time. As an 'ordinary girl' from the north without wealth or status but a steely determination to fly, she had huge popular appeal despite the reality that the 'little typist from Hull' had a degree in economics from Sheffield University. She became an instant celebrity and there was even a popular song written about her, 'Amy, Wonderful

Amy', recorded by Jack Hylton & His Orchestra. Among the many events organised to celebrate her solo flight was a lunch in her honour at the Savoy in London on 6 August 1930, arranged by the *Daily Mail*. It was described as 'A Tribute from Representatives of British Youth and Achievement in all Activities of Life'. There were many well-known figures from the world of aviation including Louis Blériot, Sir A. Verdon-Roe and Sir Sefton Brancker but also representatives of a wide range of British society and cultural interests including Brendan Bracken and Max Aitken (politics), Malcolm Sargent and John Barbirolli (music), Noël Coward and Ivor Novello (theatre and entertainment), J.B. Priestley and Evelyn Waugh (literature and journalism), Gordon Selfridge (retail), Alfred Hitchcock (cinema) and John Logie Baird (radio and television). It seemed like a recognition of the new significance of aviation well beyond its own rather closed world. Many of these figures were already wealthy or had their own celebrity status, but if they had not yet flown themselves they were almost certain to become passengers of Imperial Airways at Croydon over the next decade.

The new London airport facilities were, if anything, grander than the level of traffic required

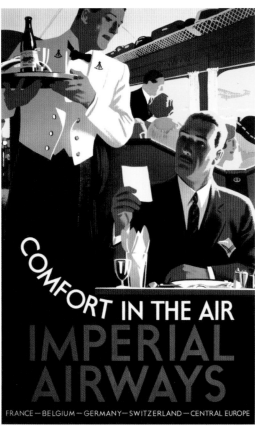

37 Comfort in the Air
Designer: Tom Purvis
Imperial Airways poster, c.1931

Dining on a Silver Wing
service was similar to a railway
restaurant car. Imperial always
emphasised comfort and luxury
rather than speed.

**38 Guide to the Airport
of London (Croydon)**
Cover designer: W.H. Scudder
Air Ministry brochure, 1931

when the terminal opened. As already mentioned, air passenger traffic in Germany was far busier than in Britain at the time, and the contemporary development of Templehof airport in Berlin was far more extensive and impressive. Templehof was closer to the city centre and despite London's claims 50 years later[44] to have opened the first metro link between a major international airport and a city centre, with the extension of the Piccadilly Underground line to Heathrow, Berlin Templehof already had an urban rail link. The centre of Berlin was easily accessible by U-bahn (the underground railway) in the 1920s, long before the massive expansion of the airport in the National Socialist period after 1933.[45]

Croydon Airport never had a direct rail link with central London and was not easily accessible from the city even in its heyday.[46] There were complaints about the state of the concrete apron around the terminal from its opening in 1928, and beyond the apron Croydon had no laid runways. Passenger aircraft were still not large or heavy enough to require runways and these never were installed at Croydon. Despite the impressive control tower and passenger departure/reception areas in the new terminal, all Croydon's take-off and landing facilities were on grass and remained fairly basic even with the introduction of radio control, lights and beacons, which made night flying possible.

**39 Imperial Airways
Atalanta**
Unknown designer
Imperial Airways poster,
*c.*1932

The Atalanta was Imperial's
first large monoplane airliner,
shown here in a desert
landing. This poster would
have been one of the last
to feature the original
Imperial winged emblem,
a conventional aero symbol
soon to be replaced by the
modernist Speedbird logo.

Flying in Print

London's prolonged juggling of its different airport sites continued in the 1930s with the development of Gatwick and Heston, but Croydon remained the hub of Imperial's operations until it was superseded by Heathrow after the war. Like Wembley's new found fame as an exhibition centre and home of major national sporting events, the name alone of this south London suburb took on an immediate romantic link with aviation. Even without publicity of its own, Croydon soon featured in everything from boys' annuals to documentary films.

'One of the most fascinating places in all the world is the immense air terminus at Croydon, just outside London' began a feature in *The Modern Boy's Book of Aircraft*, published by Fleetway in 1931. 'Aircraft start for the ends of the earth and incoming airliners land with the regularity of clockwork.' The boys' annual was edited and largely written by flying officer W.E. Johns, soon to find fame as the author of the popular Biggles stories, first published in magazines and books a year later.

The subtitle of Johns' annual is typical of the aviation publishing boom of the 1930s: *The Romance of Man's Mastery of the Skies in Picture and Story.* Other series including high-quality picture books and part-work magazines aimed mainly at boys, but also girls and interested adults, blossomed at this time. The beautifully produced *Wonder-Book* volumes published by Ward Lock featured more than 20 titles, sometimes with a new edition each year to keep up with progress. As well as *The Wonder-Book of Aircraft*, the series includes volumes on Daring Deeds, Engineering Wonders, Science, Electricity, Machinery, Motors, Ships, Railways and Empire. The *Meccano Magazine* and other popular journals made a great deal of technical and engineering achievement, especially aviation, featuring high-quality photographs and glossy coloured illustrations. The Meccano company, already famous for its eponymous construction toy and Hornby model trains, launched its popular die-cast metal Dinky Toys in the 1930s, which soon included a range of aircraft models, based on the Imperial Airways fleet, available in boxed sets. The Meccano Guild was a network of boys' clubs established by Frank Hornby, the inventor of Meccano, that stretched across the British Empire with branches in Australia, Canada, New Zealand

40 The Wonder-Book of Aircraft
Unknown designer
Cover of seventh edition, published by Ward Lock, 1931

The cover illustration shows an Imperial Airways Argosy taking off above the airport hangars. The pilot and first officer are in the high, open cockpit, with up to 20 passengers inside ready to be served luncheon on the Silver Wing service to Paris.

THE·WONDER·BOOK
OF
AIRCRAFT

41 All's Well
Illustration by Johns
Frontispiece to *The Modern Boy's Book of Aircraft*, published by Fleetway, 1931

The original picture caption reads, 'Imperial Airways pilots on the air route to Africa and India exchanging greetings from their big Short "Calcutta" flying boats.'

42 Preparing lunch in Imperial Airways liner 'Scylla'
Cigarette card issued by John Player & Sons Ltd, from an *Album of International Airliners*, c.1936.

and South Africa, all soon to be linked by Empire Air Mail.

Commercial aviation was only one part of this popular enthusiasm for new technology, but it featured very strongly in the wider culture of the 1930s and came to rival the long-held British male interest in railways. It meant that Imperial Airways had a readymade and receptive market for its own publicity when it began to develop it proactively in the 1930s. Imperial's staff started contributing photographs, technical drawings and advice to other publications, generating fantastic free publicity for the company without having to spend a great deal on direct advertising.

Everything that was published on civil aviation effectively helped to promote Imperial Airways whether officially or unofficially and in the popular market there was suddenly a great deal of coverage of the company in the 1930s. Harry Harper, a well-known journalist who liked to style himself as the first aviation correspondent and had written for many newspapers and magazines since first interviewing Blériot and the Wright brothers in 1908, teamed up with Robert Brenard, who was to become Imperial's press bureau chief, to produce *The Romance of the Flying Mail: A Pageant of Aerial Progress*. Their book, published in 1932, is a popular history of the airmail, most of which covers only the previous ten years and the creation of an Empire service. It is dedicated to 'the directors and staff of Imperial Airways, who are now establishing our British mercantile air service with traditions as fine as those which inspire our British mercantile marine'. Their last chapter is 'a final review of progress' and a paean to Imperial's achievements: 'A priceless boon to commerce, this globe-encircling flying mail should prove; while our network of world airlines, carrying their passengers as well as mails, should be something even more than that.'

43 *The Romance of the Flying Mail*
Unknown designer
Cover for a book by Harry
Harper and Robert Brenard,
published by G. Routledge
and Sons, 1932

44 Dinky Toy metal die-cast
model of an Empire Flying Boat,
1939.

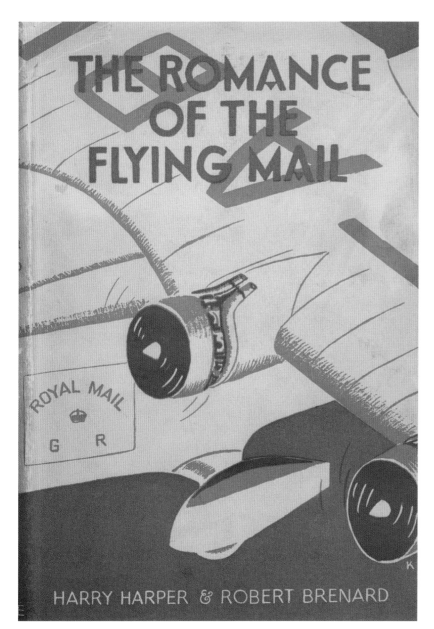

The final paragraph of the book makes a persuasive case for civilised international progress through airmail transport:

There is, truly, an immense psychological importance about the widespread development of the flying mail. And nobody realises this better than do our air-mail pilots, who are now as at home at far-distant air-stations as they are at our fine airport at Croydon. Narrow-minded views cannot survive the tolerant opinions one soon begins to form when one 'drops-in' constantly, by air mail, at towns and cities in distant lands. One's ideas cease to be national; they become international. One begins to think of one's fellow men not as citizens of any particular state, but as citizens of the world ... we now have one of the great keys to world progress of the future.[47]

A New Imperial Era

The R101 airship disaster in 1930 marked a decisive turning point in British civil aviation history. Up to that moment there were serious plans in place to develop a network of long-distance aviation routes across the Empire with airships as well as aircraft. This twin programming had probably limited the creative thinking applied to the design and development of large aircraft, but suddenly everything changed. With the loss of the R101 in northern France on 4 October the British airship programme was abandoned immediately and completely. Only six weeks after the crash, the first of a new generation of giant airliners built by Handley Page was delivered to Imperial Airways. There was no connection between the two events – the 14-ton HP42 machines had been ordered back in April 1929 – but the arrival of the new airliners seemed to confirm that aircraft were now the only way forward for civil aviation.

Breaking from the tradition of naming its aircraft after great cities, Imperial Airways gave each of the HP42s a name beginning with H derived from the history and mythology of the classical world. *Hannibal*, the first of the class, went into service on the London–Paris run in June 1931. Although small compared to an airship, it was the largest airliner in the world and widely acclaimed as the epitome of aerial comfort and elegance. The first four machines used on the European services had 38 seats. A second batch of four, starting with *Heracles*, was used on the long-distance Empire routes. These 'eastern' versions had only 18–24 seats because they needed plenty of room for the Empire Air Mail, which at this time was more important than passenger traffic.

These eight giant airliners seemed to epitomise the character of Imperial Airways in the 1930s. They looked impressive but old-fashioned even when they were first introduced, like great dragonflies on the outside and traditional railway Pullman cars inside, all polished wood, chintz and deep-cushioned seating. Not surprisingly they were slow and stately, with an alleged cruising speed of 105 mph (169 km/h), which allowed a five-course luncheon to be served on the 2.5 hour journey to Paris.

They were also exceptionally reliable and safe, with four big Bristol Jupiter engines apiece, which

45 By Air in Comfort
Designer: Steph Cavallero
Imperial Airways poster, c.1935

BY AIR IN COMFORT

TO EUROPE AFRICA ASIA BY

IMPERIAL AIRWAYS

STEPH CAVALLERO

EVERY IMPERIAL AIR LINER HAS

4 ENGINES
FOR SECURITY

IMPERIAL AIRWAYS
in 1937 carried over 70,000 passengers
and flew over 6,000,000 miles

46 Every Imperial Air Liner has 4 Engines for Security
Designer: Verney L. Danvers
Imperial Airways poster, 1938

The poster shows 'Heracles', first of the 'western' HP42s used on European routes.

INDIA

47 India
Designer: W.H.A. Constable
Imperial Airways poster, c.1933

'Hannibal' was one of the
four 'eastern' HP42s for
the Empire routes, seen flying
over Bombay.

BY IMPERIAL
AIRWAYS

IA/X 63

PRINTED IN GREAT BRITAIN STUARTS, KINGSWAY HOUSE

freight compartment in an
Heracles class 4-engine
Imperial Airways aeroplane

made landing possible even in the unlikely situation of a double engine failure. In eight years of intensive service, they were never involved in a fatal accident. The HP42s were at odds with the image of modernity that Imperial began to cultivate, and were a contrast in style with the sleek new American monoplanes that began arriving at Croydon in the mid-1930s. Nevertheless they were immensely popular with the elite group of passengers who used them and they made the new word 'air-liner' (then usually hyphenated), with all its big-ship connotations, particularly appropriate.[48]

The HP42s were literally the aerial flag-carriers of the British Empire. There was a short flagstaff above the cockpit of each aircraft from which the white ensign was flown when it was on the ground. Before departing from Croydon the co-pilot

had to open the roof hatch and retrieve the flag, which would be torn off in the air if he forgot the procedure, and on arrival at the destination airport it would be proudly flown again, anywhere from Paris Le Bourget to Karachi or Cape Town.

This little ceremony, a hangover from naval tradition, was continued by Imperial with its next generation of aircraft, but at Croydon in the late 1930s a rather different and more sinister departure routine was introduced by the German national airline. Deutsche Luft Hansa's Junkers monoplanes were the first to carry a prominent modern national symbol on the tailplane, when a large black swastika in a white disc on a red background began to appear on every aircraft, and the company agent at Croydon would see off each flight to Berlin with a Nazi salute.

IMPERIAL AIRWAYS
INGHILTERRA, ITALIA, INDIA, SUD AFRICA e AUSTRALIA

Velocità Conforto Sicurezza

50 Velocità Conforto Sicurezza (Speed Comfort Security)
Unknown designer

Imperial Airways poster, c.1935 Style would have been a more accurate word to use than speed in this Italian language poster. The photograph of models posing beside an HP42 airliner was originally taken for a fashion promotion. The Speedbird is almost lost in the poster design but it is the epitome of chic.

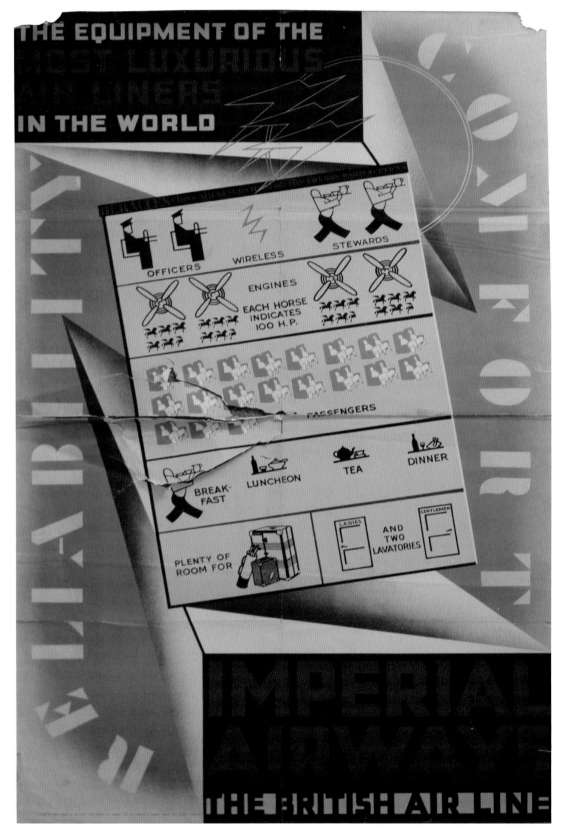

51 Reliability and Comfort
Designer: Edgar Ainsworth
Imperial Airways, c.1935

The equipment of the 'most
luxurious air liners in the world'
is promoted in pictogram and
fashionably airbrushed lettering,
all of it emphatically British.

52 Fly through Europe
Designer: Schurich
Imperial Airways poster, c.1935

A curious poster by a European
designer that might almost be
taken as a sly dig at Imperial's
old-fashioned bi-planes. An
eighteenth-century character
in periwig and tricorn hat is
surprised at the appearance
of a ghostly HP42 high above
the sailing ships of the English
Channel.

Enter the Speedbird

Between 1931 and 1938 the Imperial Airways annual publicity budget nearly doubled from £35,000 to £66,000. During this period 'publicity' at Imperial developed from the simple purchase of newspaper advertisements to the rather more sophisticated public diplomacy of producing documentary films, collaborating on the design of exhibitions in museums, galleries and other public spaces, and commissioning a range of artists, designers and writers to produce posters, leaflets and ephemera of all kinds. This was a completely new tack, and poster design finally became of great importance to the British aviation industry.

The sudden change to proactive marketing and advertising followed the appointment of C.F. 'Bill' Snowden Gamble,[49] an aviation evangelist and disciple of H.G. Wells, as Imperial Airways publicity manager. Snowden Gamble in turn appointed the Stuarts advertising agency[50] to handle Imperial's account, taking over from the tired and traditional approach of Sir Charles Higham. Marcus Brumwell[51] of Stuarts later wrote of this coup for his company: 'We studied their advertising and asserted that we could double their turnover without

increasing their appropriation. This we succeeded in doing, and in four months'[52]. The collaboration between Imperial and Stuarts was to set new visual and information standards for a decade. As *Commercial Art & Industry* magazine soon recognised, this was an ideal market match because 'the advertising of Imperial Airways presupposes a cultivated public to whom Stuart Advertising have the art of appealing'.[53]

In 1932 a striking new graphic symbol that epitomised Imperial's new approach to communication was devised through Stuarts. This was the Speedbird emblem, designed by Theyre Lee-Elliott,[54] a simple but distinctive corporate symbol that became synonymous with Imperial Airways. It soon appeared on adverts, posters, luggage labels, cigarette cards and even the stage set of a West End play by Anthony Kimmins called *The Night Club Queen*. A specially designed light blue linen material with three Speedbirds superimposed was commissioned by Imperial, advertised through its house magazine, the *Imperial Gazette*, and available through Betty Joel Limited, a fashionable interior design and furniture company.

53 Faster Empire Air Services
Designer: Ben Nicholson
Imperial Airways poster, *c*.1935

Directly commissioned by Marcus Brumwell of Stuarts, Nicholson combined his own abstract modernism with Theyre Lee-Elliott's Speedbird symbol to create a powerful new artistic image for Imperial.

FASTER EMPIRE AIR SERVICES

FLY TO

EGYPT IN 30 HOURS

SOUTH AFRICA IN 5 DAYS

INDIA IN 3 DAYS

SINGAPORE IN 5½ DAYS

AUSTRALIA IN 8 DAYS

IMPERIAL AIRWAYS

Soaring to Success !

DAILY HERALD

— the Early Bird.

Like the London Underground bar and circle 'bullseye', the much more recent Nike 'tick' logo and the Speedo swimwear symbol which closely resembles it, the Speedbird could represent Imperial Airways without lettering or explanation. It became one of the first internationally recognised brands, transcending the variations in national printing norms and vernaculars in ways that more traditional advertising did not. A trade journalist congratulated Snowden Gamble for having commissioned 'one of the most distinctive of modern symbols. It can be used on both a large and a small scale, and with a variation of colours makes a poster design that is more frequently asked for by agents than more elaborate pictorial designs.'[55]

In 1935 a leading advertising journal in the United States, *Printers' Ink Monthly*, paid tribute to the Speedbird's effectiveness in a feature headlined 'Trade Character Does an Overtime Job':

One advantage possessed by the Imperial Airways character is its agelessness. It is wholly modern in treatment, but so simple that it is difficult to conceive that it will be out of date for many years to come. Catching as it does the essence of flight, it cannot be easily outdated. By using an almost abstract conception of flight, Imperial Airways has leapt an important obstacle and has made the leap successfully. Perhaps the most notable proof of the effectiveness of the bird is that in advertisement after advertisement this trade mark, by itself or in combination with replicas of itself, serves as the only illustration and in each case the advertisement is well illustrated with the picture contributing its bit to the effectiveness of the copy.

This was praise indeed.

**54 Soaring to Success!
Daily Herald – the
Early Bird**
Designer: Edward McKnight
Kauffer
Daily Herald poster, 1919

Kauffer's strikingly Futurist
poster promoted a new
national newspaper. Its
graphic impression of flight
had no impact on Imperial
Airways publicity for more
than a decade.

Lee-Elliott, who won the 1937 'Young Achiever'
award for his design, later described how the
Speedbird evolved:

The test of a good symbol is its two-fold
ability; first, to arrest the eye and secondly
to give an indelible impression of those
characteristics it is meant to embody. In this
case those characteristics were speed and flight.

The design had to have, in my view,
a ruthless simplicity of line. The simplest
way to symbolise speed is a straight horizontal
line; flight I represented by a straight line
moving diagonally upwards. I joined these
two lines at a point and they were the bare
bones of the symbol.

As the shape had also to be reproduced as a
solid block for poster and display work, greater
substance than mere lines had to be given and
to achieve this, two further lines added to
form a shape which today we would recognise
as a fundamental 'flying wing' shape.

The remaining requirement was to give
the symbol 'character' as opposed to mere
mechanical efficiency. It was a simple matter
to 'nick' the forward edge of the horizontal
line to form a 'head' and to suggest the
change of level of a bird's wing at the shoulder,
so that the resultant shape suggested both
speed and flight in the recognisable symbol
of a bird.[56]

The Speedbird was the first application of artistic
modernism at Imperial, and a surprisingly late
introduction of design that conveys the dynamism
of flight. The symbol is a stripped down version
of an artwork first used in advertising more than
a decade earlier. The American-born artist Edward
McKnight Kauffer (1890–1954) had produced a

striking woodcut image of birds in flight at around
the time he began designing posters for the London
Underground during the First World War. His birds
were not originally intended for a poster, but the
design was reproduced in March 1919 in a launch
campaign for the left-wing newspaper, the *Daily
Herald*. Kauffer's image appeared on giant bright
yellow billboard posters above the caption 'Soaring
to Success! Daily Herald – the Early Bird'.[57]

Francis Meynell of the Nonesuch Press, who
wrote the copy and printed the *Herald* poster,
described it many years later as 'a flight of birds
that might almost be a flight of aeroplanes; a
symbol, in those days of hope, of the unity of useful
invention and natural things'.[58] The 'Flight' poster
appeared on the streets of London just as the first
post-war commercial flights were being planned,
yet nobody involved in aviation took any interest in
applying art of this kind to advertise their services.
Shortly afterwards Kauffer created a more literal
image of an aeroplane in flight for Shell Oil, but
it was for use on temporary hoardings outside the
company's head offices, not as an advertising poster.

After 1924 Imperial Airways and its advertising
agent, Charles Higham, remained apparently
disinterested in new trends in poster display, even
though Kauffer had by then become the most
successful poster designer in the country and
aviation seemed to offer obvious scope for modern
commercial artworks. Kauffer wrote at the time,
'if we used signs as a means of communication
(the aeroplane would) convey to us speed, travel,
an engine of war and terror, as well as aspiration
on the part of man to be a bird'.[59] His 'scientific'
approach to advertising with striking avant-garde
design was hotly debated in the world of commercial
art but did not have anything like universal appeal.

Lee-Elliott was a Kauffer disciple and his
Speedbird was clearly inspired by Kauffer's radical

55 Lee-Elliott's demonstration
of how his Speedbird symbol
was built up from six straight
lines, 'the result of a fortnight's
work'. Redrawn by the designer
for Imperial's publication *Air*,
April 1938 (BA Archives)

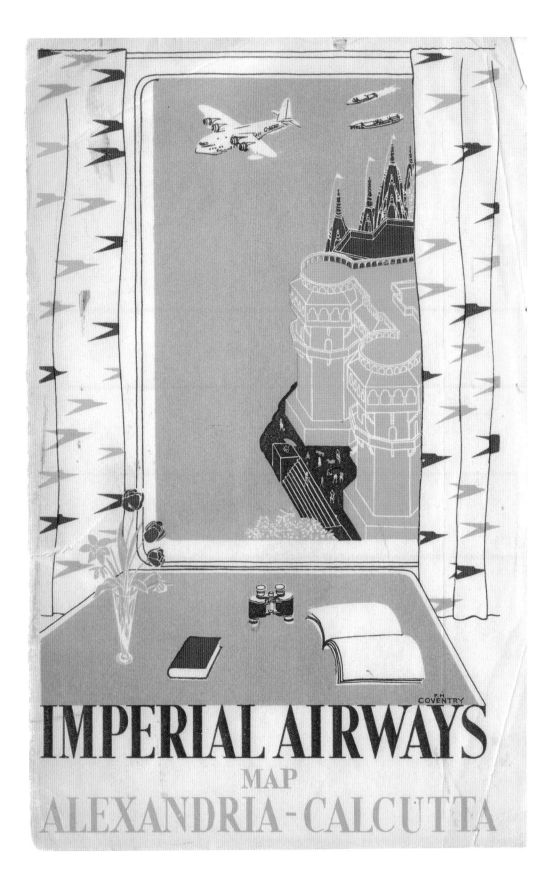

IMPERIAL AIRWAYS
MAP
ALEXANDRIA - CALCUTTA

**56 Imperial Airways Map
Alexandria–Calcutta**
Designer: Frederick Halford
Coventry
Imperial Airways passenger
leaflet cover, 1937

Maps were available to
passengers on all Imperial
Airways routes indicating
significant sights that could
be seen from the plane, either
from the passenger saloon
or, on the Empire Flying Boats,
a special observation lounge.
The Speedbird-decorated
curtain material shown here
was available to order from
interior designers Betty Joel Ltd.

57 The Empire's Airway
Designer: Theyre Lee-Elliott
London Transport poster, 1935

Lee-Elliott's poster advertises
Imperial's touring exhibition,
which opened at the Science
Museum in South Kensington,
London, before moving to
the booking hall of Charing
Cross Underground station
(now Embankment) in 1935.
It features two timeless logos,
the Imperial Speedbird and
the Underground roundel.

THE
EMPIRE'S
AIRWAY

EXHIBITION

WORKING MODELS

AND PHOTOGRAPHS

24 JUNE — 7 JULY

Open Daily 10 - 8

Admission - - Free

ORGANIZED BY
IMPERIAL
AIRWAYS

CHARING CROSS
STATION

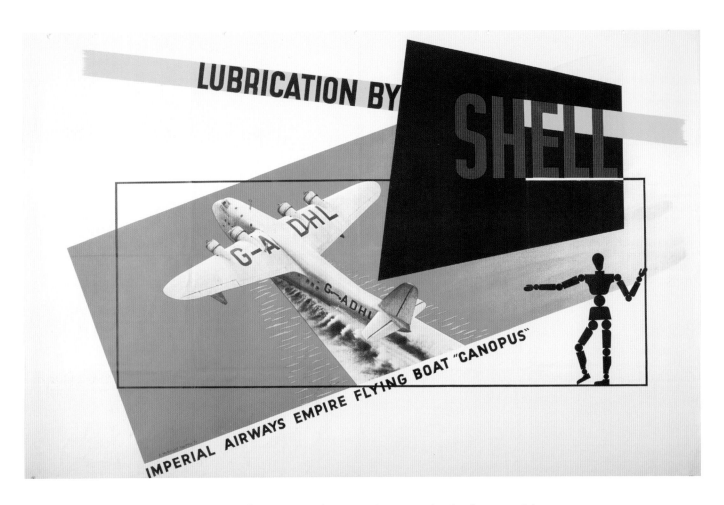

approach as well as by the jagged geometry of
Futurism. This was the main entry point for
modern design at Imperial, late in the day though
it was. Kauffer himself was soon commissioned
through Stuarts along with many other designers
that Imperial would not have considered
appropriate a few years earlier. The new approach
was encouraged by Marcus Brumwell, who had
an enthusiasm for modern art and design and knew
personally many young artists like Ben Nicholson
(1894–1982), Barbara Hepworth (1903–75) and
John Piper (1903–82). How he persuaded Snowden
Gamble, with his conservative RAF background,
to change Imperial's public image in this way
remains unclear. There is nevertheless a distinct
shift that takes place under his influence in the early
1930s, which was part of the ambiguous response
to ideas of modernism in Britain at this time.[60]

A fascinating glimpse of the internal debate
that must have taken place at Imperial Airways
on the appropriate use and style of commercial art
in publicity in this period emerges from a letter that
survives in the General Post Office (GPO) archives.
It was sent by Dennis Handover of Imperial to
Captain D.O. Lumley of the GPO in January
1933. Handover had been asked by Lumley for his
views on a proof copy of a new Air Mail poster
commissioned by the GPO from Frank Newbould
(1887–1951), one of the well-established star poster
designers for the LNER, though evidently regarded
with some suspicion by Imperial as a modernist.

Handover remarks, 'if you are paying Frank
Newbould's usual price for the poster, to my mind
you are not getting full value for the money.
This is the sort of design that would be sent by
any hack printer looking for a job to print posters.
In my view it is not nearly up to some of his other
efforts.' He goes on to criticise in planespotter-like
detail Newbould's inaccurate representation of
an Imperial Atalanta aircraft in his stylised artwork

59 Le Touquet One Flying Hour
Designer: Theyre Lee-Elliott
Imperial Airways poster, c.1935

Le Touquet in northern France became a fashionable resort for those who wanted a quick air trip for a pricey weekend break at the seaside.

IMPERIAL AIRWAYS

FLY FROM
ENGLAND
TO INDIA IN
6
DAYS
VIA EGYPT 'IRAQ

LEE-ELLIOTT

**60 Fly from England
to India in 6 Days**
Designer: Theyre Lee-Elliott
Imperial Airways poster, c.1935

The poster as image-builder
rather than ticket-seller.
The six-day journey to India
was more to do with speeding
up the mail than reducing
passenger journey times. In
fact, Imperial was carrying only
about 75 paying passengers
a year from Croydon to India
at this time, every one of
them heavily subsidised, but
airmail services revolutionised
communications across the
British Empire where the
journey from England to India
still took six weeks by boat.

61 Use the Air Mail
Designer: Frank Newbould
General Post Office poster,
1933

Newbould's stylised airliner
in this GPO poster prompted
a sharp response from Imperial.

('insufficient windows ... blue line should stop dead at the tailplane'). The letter ends with a slightly barbed request for closer cooperation between Imperial and the GPO:

> Why should not the Post Office give a little credit to its national Company by putting the name 'Imperial Airways' on the aircraft as it appears in real life? It would not do any harm, and I do not think the Post Office would be ashamed to give a very small advertisement to this Company, neither would it offend any of the departmental regulations. Possibly a reminder of this point will allow you to insert it in some way.[61]

A copy of Lumley's reply, if he sent one, does not survive, but this single letter is indicative of the cultural changes that both Imperial and the GPO were grappling with at this time. Stuarts had only just taken on Imperial's advertising and was not involved in this exchange. Meanwhile the Post Office was feeling its way with one of its first poster commissions, and had not yet established a clear policy for managing artists and designers. There is a real sense of flux in both organisations.

By 1937, Brumwell was commissioning a leaflet for Imperial passengers from John Piper with a completely abstract cover design headlined 'Modern Travel for Modern People'. Inside the publication, Piper offered his own view on the 'modern art' that so many people found baffling:

> My intention in doing a painting is not to imitate anything but to originate something. I have tried to make a bright design that will catch your eye and make you wonder what is inside this book. People usually want to 'understand the meaning' of pictures. Why?

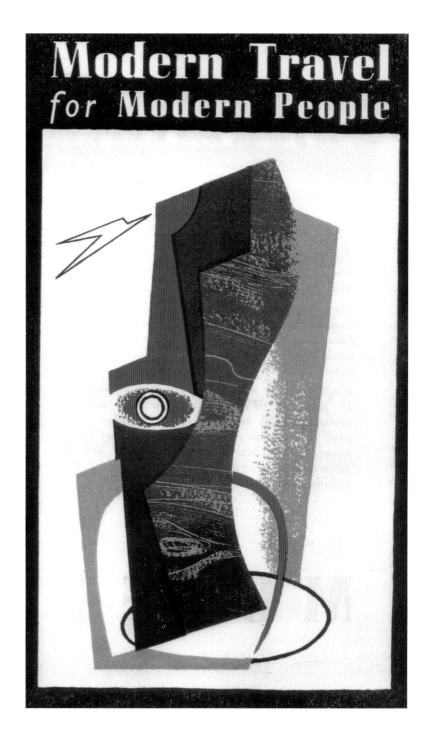

62 Modern Travel for Modern People
Designer: John Piper
Imperial Airways passenger leaflet, c.1937

Knowing your market: an Imperial leaflet artfully aimed at passengers who already considered themselves modern people with taste.

They do not ask to understand the meaning
of the enjoyment of good food, country air
or the colour of beech leaves in autumn
– they do not even ask to understand the
irritation of wet weather at the seaside.[62]

This is as far removed from traditional advertising
copy as it could be.

The Speedbird became the central motif for
nearly all publicity at Imperial and was incorporated
in the work of other designers, though Lee-Elliott
was personally responsible for a good deal of it
himself. The only place the Speedbird did not
appear until the late 1930s was on Imperial's aircraft,
suggesting either a residual conservatism on the
operational side or, more likely, that it was seen to
work best in a more dynamic, streamlined context.

There was a very short lead time for producing
and printing new publicity, but introducing
new aircraft followed months of design, research
and construction. When the Speedbird was
adopted, Imperial had only just taken delivery of its
HP42 bi-planes, which already looked antiquated.
Appropriately, the symbol was only applied to
the fuselage of Imperial's first aerodynamic
machines, the Frobisher class airliners which were
delivered from 1938. The symbol looked far more
appropriate on the clean, sleek bodywork of what
were then, briefly, the fastest commercial airliners
in the world.

The six new aircraft were in commercial service
for less than a year because of the outbreak of war
but the Speedbird symbol was carried by every
plane in the fleet of Imperial's successor BOAC
throughout the war and beyond. The Speedbird
was retained as the corporate symbol when the
modern British Airways (BA) was created in 1974
and only finally abandoned ten years later when
BA prepared for privatisation and adopted a new

63 *Fingal*, one of the elegant
new Frobisher class airliners,
sports the Imperial Speedbird
on its fuselage at Croydon,
1939.

64 *Imperial Airways
in Pictures*
Photographer: Jarche
Cover of a stylish photographic
record of Imperial's operations
produced by Stuarts as
corporate publicity, 1938.

visual identity. The Speedbird was replaced by
the Speedwing, which in turn was changed to the
stylised ribbon-shape of the current Speedmarque
in 1997. Speedbird still survives on the airwaves
as it is used as the call sign for all BA aircraft during
air traffic control procedures.

The Art of Good Design

65 Globe and Map
Designer: James Gardner
Imperial Airways poster, 1938

Gardner was probably the
first designer to adapt the idea
of the stylised route diagram
used by Harry Beck in his
iconic London Underground
map of 1933 to the broader
canvas of international airline
routes. This poster appeared
only five years later, long
before diagrams became
standard practice for airlines.

New design standards were not applied rigidly
across Imperial Airways in the 1930s and it would
be misleading to describe the work that was
undertaken with Stuarts and others as a corporate
identity programme. There is a range, diversity
and creativity about it that would be hard to find in
a modern business, whether a large private company
or a public corporation. To some extent this reflects
a particular characteristic of 1930s Britain, when art
and industry briefly came together in a number of
organisations and individual projects with striking
results, ranging from the interior design of the
Queen Mary, Cunard's flagship ocean liner, to
the creation of pioneering documentary films like
Night Mail (1936) for the Post Office.

What might be described as practical and
applied artistic creativity flourished across the
board, encouraged by committed individuals
like Frank Pick, who found time to combine the
new role of chief executive at London Transport
from 1933 with becoming, a year later, the first
chairman of the government's new Council for Art
and Industry, forerunner of the Design Council.
Pick was determined to spread the gospel of

'fitness for purpose' preached by the Design and
Industries Association (DIA) and push for high
design standards throughout British commerce and
industry. He was in a particularly strong position
to do this.[63]

Another influential figure who made an
immediate impact at this time was Jack Beddington
(1893–1959), who became publicity director for
Shell Oil in 1932. Like Pick he was, in Ruth
Artmonsky's phrase, 'one of the twentieth century
Medici, organisational sponsors of the applied
visual arts'.[64] Like Snowden Gamble, Beddington
quickly dispensed with the services of the large
and ineffectual American advertising agency with
whom Shell had been working and appointed
Stuarts instead. He shared with Brumwell at Stuarts
an interest in commissioning innovative young
artists whose work he admired and Shell gave him
a free hand to do this.

Shell had produced some memorable advertising
before Beddington took over, but he introduced a
much wider range, including the work of artists who
had rarely if ever ventured into commercial design
before. One of the first 'lorry bills' commissioned

**66 Travel in Comfort
by Imperial Airways**
Designer: Edward McKnight
Kauffer
Imperial Airways poster, *c.*1935

Kauffer, whose own work
had inspired Lee-Elliot to create
the Speedbird, incorporated the
new logo in a series of designs
for Imperial commissioned by
Stuarts from 1933.

67 For Reliability, Shell Lubricating Oil
Designer: Barnett Freedman
Shell poster, 1932

One of the first 'lorry bill' posters commissioned by Jack Beddington at Shell promoted Imperial's latest monoplane airliner as much as Shell's lubricating oil.

FOR RELIABILITY-

G-ABPI

ATALANTA CLASS AIR LINER

BARNETT FREEDMAN

SHELL LUBRICATING OIL

by Beddington, which were not displayed on hoardings but on the side panels of Shell delivery trucks, was by the lithographer Barnett Freedman (1901–58), whose work he particularly championed. The poster depicts a new Atalanta airliner, Imperial's latest aircraft in flight in 1932. This widely viewed publicity, seen all over the country, would have been as useful to the airline as it was to Shell, Imperial's main fuel supplier.[65]

In 1934 Beddington was instrumental in setting up the Shell film unit, although accounts of how this came about vary.[66] Significantly this was also closely associated with Imperial, as the Shell unit's first film was *Airport*, a well-received documentary about a day in the life of Croydon Airport. Shell's reputation was enhanced by association with the glamour of flying and Imperial got more free publicity. This was the softest of public relations campaigns and typical of Beddington's quietly effective approach, which was much admired by artists, film-makers and advertisers. It was no surprise that in 1940 he was made director

68 Loading the Air Mails
Designer: H.S. Williamson
General Post Office poster for
schools, 1934

One of the first GPO posters for
schools was this view of a Short
Scylla being loaded with airmail
at Croydon.

LOADING AIR MAILS FOR THE EMPIRE: CROYDON. 1934

of the films division in the wartime Ministry of Information.

Visual publicity through the medium of posters and film was widely used to do more than sell products and services. For Imperial, and the aviation evangelists like Snowdon Gamble and Robert Brenard within it, this was about promoting the concept of air transport and communication as the key to future life across the Empire Air Mail routes. The short-term business benefits of selling an immediate advertising product, whether a passenger ticket or an airmail package, was less significant. The artists and designers commissioned by Stuarts on Imperial's behalf were effectively

69 Pages from an Imperial Airways brochure
Illustrators: James Gardner (left); Rowland Hilder (right) c.1939.

The details show size comparisons between an Empire Flying Boat and a London bus, and between the new Ensign airliner and a mounted policeman.

contributing to both. It was not generous artistic patronage without strings, but neither was it art used for commercial profit in cheap advertising.

Imperial Airways faced a similar issue to another, much larger public service organisation in the 1930s, the General Post Office. With the progressive development of airmail services the GPO was also concerned to promote new facilities to the public but fought shy of commercial advertising. In 1933, when the Empire Marketing Board was closed and its secretary Stephen Tallents (1884–1958) moved to the GPO, he set up a public relations department there which considered ways to publicise its role and services more effectively. Tallents brought with him the EMB film unit under John Grierson, which now became the GPO film unit.

The GPO was quite different in scale and complexity to the EMB. The GPO was responsible for running a vast nationwide government service rather than a small state marketing and propaganda unit. But the scope for selling ideas to the nation

by engaging with the new media of the day (posters and film) was appealing to GPO managers struggling to reorganise and modernise its complex operations. The Director of Postal Services, Sir Frederick Williamson, suggested that it might be a good idea to 'familiarise the youthful mind with the possibilities of air services'.[67]

Two posters were commissioned in 1934 specifically for use in schools rather than public display. This was a modest start that grew into an extensive publicity programme. Although there was a network of post offices all over the country, suitable sites for displaying posters were limited. The GPO could not use its own buildings and public environments for advertising in the way that the railways and the Underground could, but it obviously had the resources on hand to send posters to schools and other institutions.

One of the first pair of posters designed for school use on the theme of 'Overseas Communications' showed the loading of airmail on to an Imperial airliner at Croydon. It was designed by Harold Sandys Williamson (1892–1978), principal of the Chelsea School of Art. He was a well-established graphic designer who had produced a number of posters for Pick at the London Underground. Tallents had used Pick's advice in commissioning posters for the EMB, and he now set up an advisory committee for publicity at the GPO which included Jack Beddington, the art critic Clive Bell and Kenneth Clark, the young director of the National Gallery, who also happened to be a close friend and admirer of Edward McKnight Kauffer.

The web of overlapping relationships created in this period between artists, designers and semi-public institutions through key individuals like Pick, Tallents and Beddington is at first sight quite astonishing. Today it might look deeply suspect, like the dominance of an artistic, intellectual clique promoted by a handful of influential executives exercising their personal taste. It would certainly not meet modern expectations of competition, transparency or tendering in the provision of services. However, none of these individuals were driven by financial gain or likely to enrich themselves through such patronage. The social and cultural value of enlightened artistic commissions in industry and commerce that blossomed in the 1930s far outweighed the cost, which was modest all round. The number of committed and visionary publicity managers, the size of intermediary advertising agencies and the pool of skilled artistic and design talent were all small, so it is no surprise that they overlapped and interconnected. What is surprising is that so much was achieved in this area by so few people in this troubled decade. Tallents only stayed at the GPO for two years before moving on to the BBC, where he was put in charge of public relations for another arm's-length public corporation.

The scope for collaboration with Imperial Airways in promoting airmail services was obvious, as the tetchy correspondence about Newbould's earlier poster suggests. Lee-Elliott was asked to devise new graphic symbols and publicity for Air Mail and, along with Kauffer and other leading graphic designers, he designed striking posters for what became in effect a joint public service operation. Up to the mid-1930s all mail carried by air was subject to a surcharge, which meant that the bulk of overseas mail still went by rail and ship. Under the Empire Air Mail Scheme agreed in 1935, Imperial Airways were allowed to carry all types of mail between Empire countries with no surcharge. Two years later airmail surcharges were abolished for internal and European services. The result was an astonishing tenfold increase in first-class external letter mail and the benefits of promoting the service were clear.

Artists and film-makers were soon working with Imperial Airways and the GPO on a range of projects. A cycle of documentary films produced by Paul Rotha was allocated a particularly important role in the creation of Imperial's public image. *African Skyways* (1939), directed by Donald Taylor, is a typical example, detailing the developmental impact of Imperial's services, its operations on the ground and the passengers it carries. The film's opening section positions British civil aviation as a crucial link between disparate peoples. With the camera providing a panoramic view of Cairo, the voiceover praises the 'fine arterial roads', trains, trams and modern social services of the Egyptian capital, but a few minutes later we are shown that in the countryside 'little has changed since the time of the pharaohs'. Though the film's representation of Egyptian peasants is sensitive, there is a palpable impatience to it. There is an unmistakable implication that the plane should be succeeding

70 **Africa by Imperial Airways**
Designer: Hal Woolf
Imperial Airways poster, *c.*1934

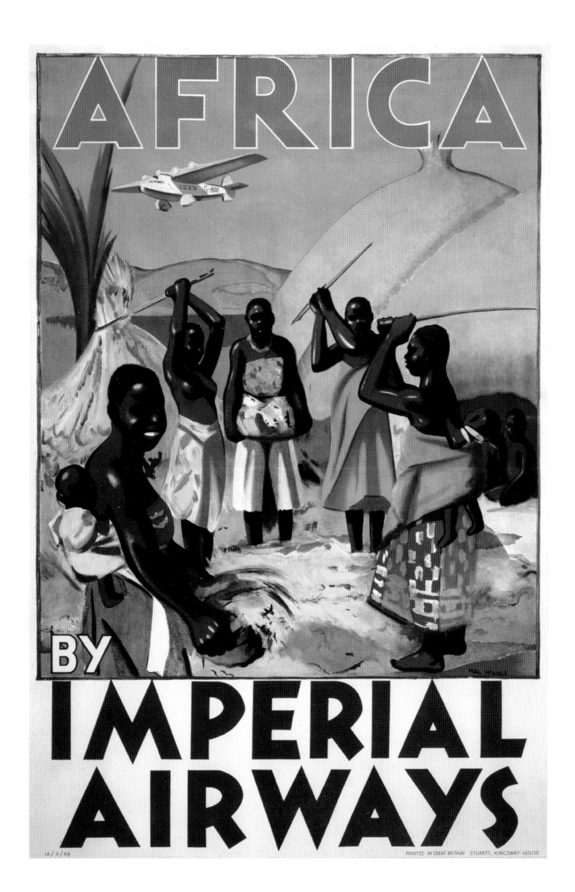

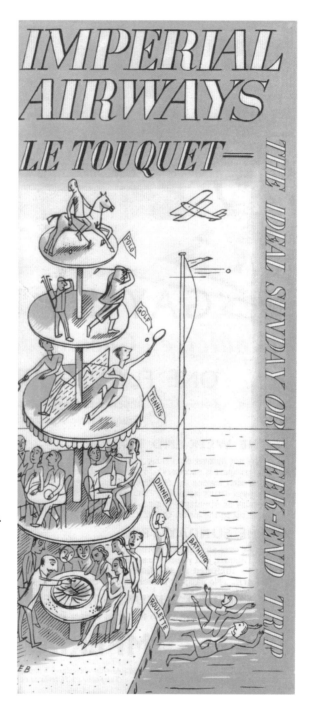

the Nile as Egypt's main highway. Air travel was
resurrecting Cecil Rhodes' Victorian colonial dream
of constructing a trade route from Cairo to the Cape.

Like the contemporary Soviet propaganda
films of the 'Five year plan in four years' era, the
Imperial Airways films of the 1930s carry a frenetic
development message that sees the aeroplane
succeeding the elephant track. *African Skyways*
looks at agricultural colleges and new industry.
'It is scarcely too much to say that Tanganyika may
never really know the stagecoach,' says Imperial's
African spokesman. 'The leap that was taken here
in East Africa in a very few years was in Europe

and other continents a slow, dragging process of centuries.' The inter-war imperial narrative hops by aeroplane between dimensions of the past, present and future.[68]

Time was an important trope in all Imperial Airways publicity. Pragmatically, Imperial promised to reduce the time wasted in transit by both businessmen and the communication links between businesses. Less tangibly, Imperial Airways publicity continually emphasised how aviation was reshaping global geography (pilots are invariably described as 'travellers in time and space') and that this physical reconfiguration had political consequences.

Naval strength had underpinned Britain's rise to global prominence, while aviation promised to determine Britain's place in the 'coming world economic unit of the future'. Undeniably the development of European aviation was animated by both national and international competition, but aviation proved an intrinsically internationalist technology requiring pan-national legal, technical and organisational standards. It was a technology of diplomats and technicians rather than explorers and speculators. Indeed, Imperial underwrote the establishment of Indian Trans-Continental Airlines and QANTAS in Australia, and an influential strand of liberal thought of the period further pressed for the creation of an international air police force.

Bill Snowden Gamble's wider intellectual vision was for Imperial to blend art, education and technology, enabling every citizen to become 'a true democrat'.[69] This did not mean everyone travelling on his aircraft, but Imperial could make a huge difference. 'In the future,' Gamble said, paraphrasing H.G. Wells in *A Short History of the World*, aviation would enable the human race to go 'from strength to strength in an ever splendid circle of adventure and achievement'[70]. Gamble saw it as Imperial's task to help develop the visual language of an emerging international psychology. The aesthetic and intellectual ambition of Imperial's advertising reflected the organisation's lack of an immediate public constituency and, with little pressure to sell tickets, Gamble was able to sell ideals.[71]

Brumwell brought a wide range of creative talent to this mission for Imperial through Stuarts, commissioning artists and designers. They produced everything from abstract modern artworks like the posters of Lee-Elliott and Nicholson to the humorous illustrations in travel guides and brochures by Edward Bawden

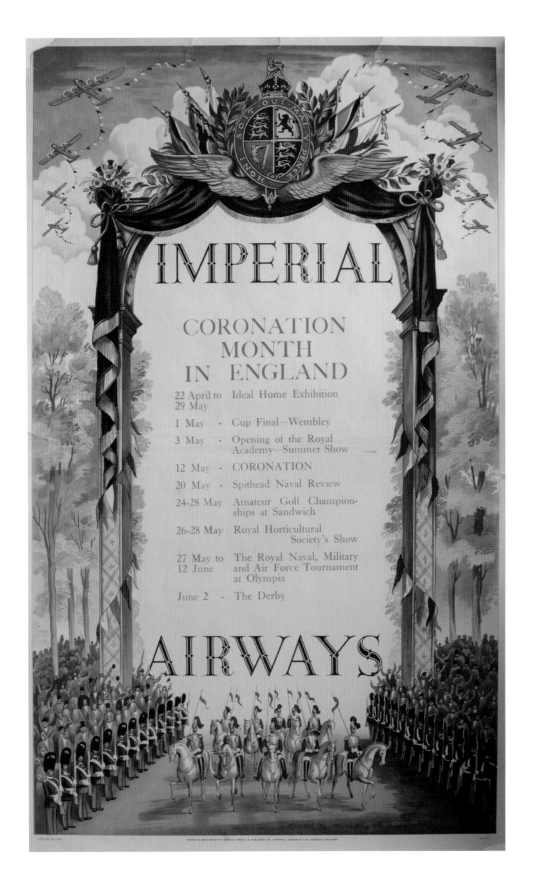

74 Coronation Month in England
Designer: Rex Whistler
Imperial Airways poster, 1937

Whistler's special design for the coronation of George VI was used to frame a whole range of Imperial Airways announcements and activities in 1937 including foreign language printings.

(1903–89) and Rex Whistler (1905–44), who had produced similar work for, amongst others, the London Underground, Shell-Mex and Fortnum & Mason. Since graduating from the Royal College of Art in the early 1920s, the prolific Bawden had almost established a niche market for commercial illustration work, and his designs for Imperial applied to passenger maps, guides and an elaborate 'Certificate of Contemporary Travel' given out on the Empire Flying Boats were all in his characteristic quirky style. One of them was used to headline a major article on his work in *Art and Industry* magazine in 1937 which claimed that although his name was not well known, 'Bawden's art has insinuated itself into manifold aspects of our everyday life.'[72]

Rex Whistler was another artist whose style was more recognisable than his name. He had famously created a long, decorative mural round the walls of the Tate Gallery's restaurant in 1927, when he was just 22. Use of the artwork had immediately reached well beyond the art gallery audience when it was reproduced by Frank Pick as an Underground poster. A year later Whistler started producing drawings for Shell press advertisements, which soon included his popular, comic 'reversible head' series.

Jack Beddington, when he took over Shell's publicity, recognised that these caricatures were the least of Whistler's artistic skills and commissioned from him a fine landscape view of the Vale of Aylesbury. This became one of Shell's famous lorry bill posters. Meanwhile, Stuarts asked Whistler to design a suitably prestigious poster for Imperial, which could be used to promote the coronation celebrations for George VI in May 1937. This was, of course, the first coronation to which overseas visitors or Britons living abroad might fly to London in a luxury airliner. Whistler's decorative poster design appeared with various printed

75 A Certificate of Contemporary Travel
Designer: Edward Bawden
Imperial Airways illustrated certificate, 1937

Bawden's beautifully illustrated 'Certificate of Contemporary Travel', printed on high quality card, was available to all Empire Flying Boat passengers. It would be signed personally by the flight captain, who would come back into the cabin to greet all his passengers personally.

76 The Empire's Airway
Designer: László Moholy-Nagy
Cover to Imperial Airways
Science Museum exhibition
leaflet, 1935

76 The Empire's Airway
Designer: László Moholy-Nagy
Cover to Imperial Airways
Science Museum exhibition
leaflet, 1935

messages, including one with the text in French. Always rather less meticulous than Bawden in his commercial dealings, Whistler did not sign or even initial his original artwork and the printed posters in BA's archives have only recently been identified as his work.[73]

Other designers got new opportunities at Imperial through Stuarts. James Gardner (1901–95), who later recalled that one of his first 3D design jobs for Imperial Airways was for an aircraft toilet, produced superb airbrushed illustrations for

Imperial booklets and brochures in the late 1930s. He was probably the first designer to recognise the scope for adapting the diagrammatic principle of the new London tube map to international airline routes in one of his striking posters for Imperial in 1938. After the war Gardner became a leading exhibition designer, responsible for the *Britain Can Make It* exhibition at the Victoria and Albert Museum in 1946, displays at the Festival of Britain and the interior hall of the Commonwealth Institute in 1962.[74]

77 Flying over the Empire
Designer: Theyre Lee-Elliott
Cover to Imperial Airways
travelling exhibition of aerial and
infra-red photography, 1934

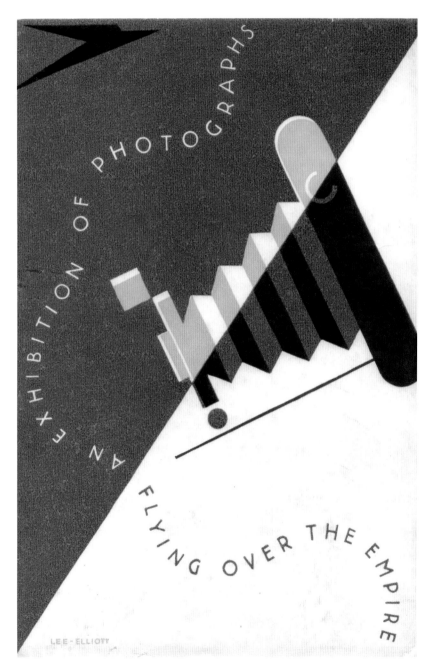

The avant-garde Hungarian designer László
Moholy-Nagy (1895–1946), who had taught at
the original German Bauhaus in Dessau, was one
of many émigré artists who moved to London
after the Nazis came to power in 1933. One of his
first pieces of freelance work in England was for
Imperial and would have come through Stuarts.
Moholy-Nagy was the graphic designer and
photographer for *The Empire's Airway*, a stylish
modernist exhibition mounted at the Science
Museum in South Kensington in 1935. This was
a complete departure from the traditional forms
of museum display presentation. It included
axonometric drawings, specially made display
models and large photomontage panels, features
that were commonplace in the 1960s but years
ahead of their time in 1930s London. An adapted
version of the display was presented six months later
in the booking hall of Charing Cross Underground
station, which London Transport made available for
public exhibitions at this time. This was advertised
with a special Underground poster designed by
Lee-Elliott featuring the graphic symbols of both
organisations, the London Transport bullseye and
his Imperial Speedbird.

Imperial had first experimented with an
'artistic' exhibition in 1934 when a collection
of more than 100 photographs called *Flying over
the Empire* had been shown in a Bond Street gallery.
The most arresting of these was a series of infra-red
pictures (then quite a novel technique) taken
from the air along the Empire routes to the Far
East and through Africa. They were specially taken
by staff photographers from *The Times*, which
promoted the show and later sent it on tour to
provincial galleries.

The well-known art and design critic Herbert
Read, an outspoken champion of modern artists like
Ben Nicholson and Paul Nash, provided a foreword

to the catalogue. He was fascinated by the beauty of the infra-red images but also suggested that:

> the aeroplane in itself has become a thing of beauty; compare the types of 1924 and 1934 and note how well the lines of the latest models compose into an expressive pattern – a pattern not only of swift flight and clean efficiency, but even of some more absolute quality which is common to all great art. When a design of such beauty is photographed in the air against a background of clouds and space, the result gives us an aesthetic experience of a totally new kind.[75]

As well as the documentary films produced for Imperial by Paul Rotha, and those made in collaboration with the Shell and GPO film units, there were the experimental, almost psychedelic productions of Len Lye such as *Colour Flight*, an innovative short film made in 1937 without the use of a camera. It featured swing music, with colours and shapes painted directly on to clear film. Imperial's press release for the film describes how:

> the shape, the sound and the colour make a single exhilarating rhythm ... trumpet notes dance in greenish whirlwinds across a background of purple and violet. The shape of the Imperial Airways Speedbird symbol appears. Singly, in twos and threes, in flocks, they drift and wheel across chromatic skies, shoot off on interplanetary voyages, circling Saturn and his rings. Letter by letter, like a mechanical neon sign, the slogan FLY IMPERIAL AIRWAYS spells itself out in jazz time.

Lye himself said simply that it was 'made primarily as a propaganda film to include a few slogans. It remains primarily entertainment exploiting new film ground'. *Colour Flight*, together with the films *Wings over Empire* and *Sydney Eastbound*, were among the exhibits chosen to represent Imperial Airways and Britain at the New York World's Fair in 1939–40.

More conventional but widely accessible publicity for Imperial was organised by Stuarts with regular articles placed in *The Times*, often written for the newspaper by Imperial's managing director, Woods Humphery, or delivered as lectures and then reproduced as offprints in brochures. These were aimed at opinion formers and politicians as a way of building support for new civil aviation policies favourable to Imperial, but there were other initiatives aimed at enthusing a wider public. A set of lantern slides with descriptive notes could be borrowed free of charge by anyone wanting to present a show to a local club or society meeting, a publicity feature copied from London Transport. The aviation films were also available on loan for presentation to clubs and societies. There was even an Imperial Airways exhibition train that toured the country offering free shows in stations and railway depots. The art and design that went into this was astonishingly varied and diverse, highly creative and yet expertly blended together to create a clear and powerful public vision.

Unfortunately Imperial's considerable publicity achievements were somewhat undermined in its final years by bruising management battles, administrative problems and ultimately a crisis of political confidence in the way the company was being run. Its next ambitious development plan for a transatlantic passenger service by flying boat was overtaken by the outbreak of war and never actually achieved. No amount of skilfully applied art and design or upbeat publicity could overcome these practical problems and a deteriorating international situation in Europe and beyond.

78 Fly from Iraq
Designer: Ben Nicholson
Imperial Airways poster, *c*.1935

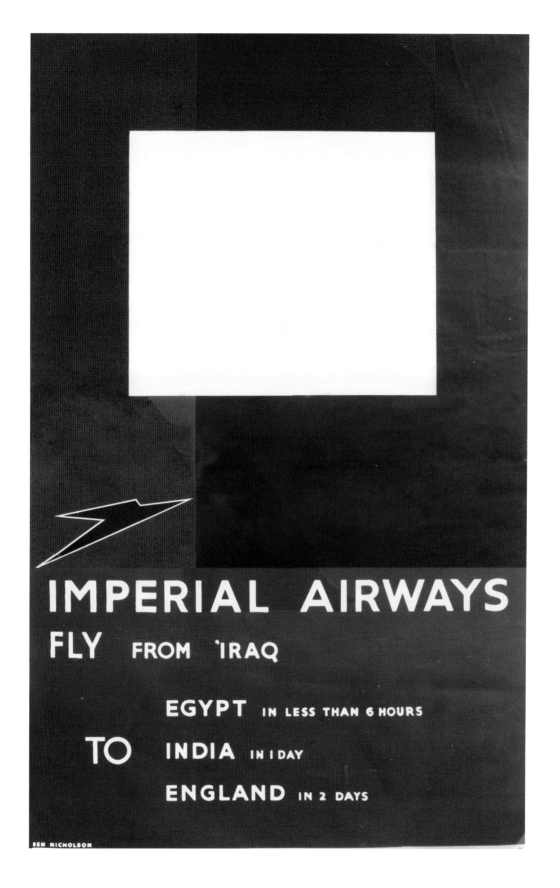

IMPERIAL AIRWAYS
FLY FROM 'IRAQ

EGYPT IN LESS THAN 6 HOURS
TO INDIA IN 1 DAY
ENGLAND IN 2 DAYS

BEN NICHOLSON

The End of Empire

By the mid-1930s Imperial had come a long way. Route mileage flown had increased from just 1,520 in its first year of operation to just over 15,500 in 1935. Passenger traffic was up from 10,321 to 66,324. In 1935 it made an operational profit of £140,705 and the subsidy from government was down to less than 28 per cent of its income. Yet the statistics, as always, could be read in different ways. Without subsidy payments of nearly £600,000 in 1935 Imperial would have been making a substantial loss, and there was no chance of the airline becoming financially self-sufficient as had been hoped back in 1924.

In 1936, 55 per cent of the total passenger mileage flown by the company was on Empire routes but it accounted for only 10 per cent of the passengers carried. A continuing government policy of encouraging imperial communications tended to retard development elsewhere, particularly in Europe. As a result, non-Empire routes were neglected. In Europe, there was no British service east of Cologne and not one British night airmail service out of the country.[76]

These deficiencies apparently stemmed from government policy rather than failures at Imperial Airways. Without more resources, Imperial could hardly be expected to develop its European services as well as maintaining the new Empire routes and introducing the Empire Air Mail scheme. Meanwhile, a number of small, unsubsidised and independent airlines that were developing domestic routes merged together in 1935 to create British Airways Ltd,[77] initially to compete with Imperial on short-haul services. With the ten-year exclusive state subsidy of Imperial now expired, the government decided to make British Airways its second 'chosen instrument', entrusting it with subsidised air routes in Europe, but with fewer restrictions. Crucially, British Airways was not hamstrung with Imperial's continued obligation to buy British and quickly ordered some sleek American Lockheed Electra airliners for its new European services.[78] At the same time the Air Navigation Act (1936) provided new and additional financial aid to Imperial, raising its subsidy limit to £1.5 million a year.

Imperial had already chosen to develop its long-distance routes, including the Empire Air

79 28 'Hydravions' Empire Neufs/28 New 'Empire' Flying Boats
Designer: Albert Brenet
Imperial Airways poster, 1937

French poster artist Brenet created a distinctly sinister and prophetic image with his mass of new Empire Flying Boats darkening the sky like a fleet of bombers. Three years later the Luftwaffe began its nightly mass raids with the London Blitz.

80 British Airways
Unknown designer
British Airways poster, c.1936

A poster for the new British Airways Ltd (not to be confused with the latter-day British Airways) featuring one of its reliable small airliners for domestic and European services, the DH86.

81 Cologne Leipzig Prague Vienna Budapest
Unknown designer
Imperial Airways poster, 1935

Imperial's limited East European service offered new market opportunities for the upstart rival British Airways in the

mid-1930s, but all these routes were soon disrupted as Nazi Germany threatened to destabilise the Continent. The plane used by Imperial was the small DH.86 Express airliner, which had just 10 seats. These were the last of the British commercial bi-planes.

82 Empire Flying Boat
Designer: Mark Severin
Imperial airways poster, 1937

The Empire Flying Boats were progressively introduced from 1937 and all 28 had been delivered by 1939. The new fleet operated successfully

on the existing Empire routes but a transatlantic passenger service could not be introduced before the war.

Mail scheme and transatlantic services to Canada and the United States, primarily with flying boats. To do this they needed a fleet of fast, modern aircraft. No suitable prototype had been developed, but in a huge leap of faith Imperial placed a £1.75 million order with Short Brothers of Rochester in 1934 to design and build 28 state-of-the-art flying boats straight off the drawing board. This was the company's largest single order for new aircraft, known by Imperial as its C class seaplanes but soon to become famous as the classic Empire Flying Boats, with names like *Canopus*, *Caledonia* and *Cambria*.[79]

As one historian has rightly observed, 'the Empire boats were the first civil aircraft in Britain to show a healthy respect for smooth lines and cutting edge aerodynamics ... these aeroplanes were unashamedly modern and yet reassuringly secure, contriving to be both streamlined and solid'.[80] While land planes continued to use Croydon, Southampton became the operational centre for Imperial's seaplanes. *Castor* landed in the Solent with the first scheduled service, bringing 15 passengers and an airmail delivery from Alexandria in March 1937. Three months later the Empire Mail Programme was inaugurated right through eastern and southern Africa, and soon afterwards trials for transatlantic mail services were under way. Imperial's posters and other publicity made the most of these impressive developments, in which British civil aviation was proving as advanced as the United States and covering greater distances across the globe than any other European nation.

Yet at the same time Imperial was facing persistent criticism in parliamentary debates with serious accusations of official incompetence and inefficiency. A committee under Lord Cadman set up to investigate the state of Britain's civil aviation issued an unusually critical official report

in March 1938. Both Imperial and the Air Ministry were castigated for poor future planning and cooperation, which had left the national airline with an obsolete fleet and inadequate resources to develop: 'If, as we assume, the Government desire this country to take a leading place in civil aviation, much reorganisation and additional expenditure of public money will be necessary.'[81]

Astonishingly, the government accepted Cadman's recommendation that the subsidy limit on Imperial Airways should be doubled immediately to £3 million. In June 1938, a new full-time chairman was appointed for the company, and he quickly made his own proposal for restructuring the state airline businesses. The new chairman was Sir John Reith (1889–1971), who was persuaded to leave the top job at the BBC to sort out Imperial. With his experience in setting up one of the first and most successful public corporations in the country, it was not surprising

83 Prime Minister Neville Chamberlain returns to Heston from Munich after his third meeting with Hitler, clutching his 'peace in our time' appeasement agreement, September 1938. Chamberlain, who had never flown before making three visits to Germany in a month, flew in a brand new British Airways Lockheed Electra.

IMPERIAL AIRWAYS → THE FROBISHERS FASTEST BRITISH AIR LINERS
EUROPE · AFRICA · INDIA · THE FAR EAST · AUSTRALIA · U.S.A. - BERMUDA   4 ENGINES · SPEED WITH COMFORT

84 The Frobishers
Unknown designer
Imperial Airways poster, 1939

An impressive cutaway of
one of the elegant Frobishers
that went into service from
December 1938. All of these
planes were withdrawn
when war broke out nine
months later.

that Reith brought to civil aviation what one
historian has described as 'the gospel of a single
chosen instrument exercising public responsibility
for an industry dependent on public money'.[82]

Reith's scheme was to merge Imperial and British
Airways into a single national air corporation.
A Conservative government, swayed by the
deteriorating international situation in Europe,
took Reith's proposal for nationalisation forward
and brought it to the House of Commons in the
summer of 1939. In April 1940 the British Overseas
Airways Corporation (BOAC) formally came into
being, taking over both airlines and a mixed bag of
69 aircraft of 13 different types. By this time Britain
had been at war for eight months. Once again,
international events had completely overtaken the
development of peaceful civil aviation. All existing
passenger services had been suspended in September
1939 and Imperial's staff, who had only just
moved into the swish new headquarters building

in Victoria, London, in July, were immediately
evacuated to Bristol. For the duration of the war
aircraft, staff and operations were put at the disposal
of the Air Ministry and, as Reith confided to his
diary, 'completely subordinated to the military'.

A schedule of 'normal' civilian services would
not be possible for the next six years, although
numerous unarmed transport and delivery
services were operated by BOAC aircraft and staff
throughout the war. By 1945–6 everything to do
with aviation had changed out of all recognition,
with even faster technological development born
of wartime necessity and military experience.
Post-war civil aviation plans would require a new
start with a blank sheet in austerity conditions and
a Labour government committed to the wholesale
nationalisation of British industry. BOAC's
immediate task was to rebuild its route network
and prepare for the inevitable commercial struggle
ahead, but with no clear road map to the future.

Conflict and a Changing World

OLIVER GREEN

BOAC's first five years' operation from 1940 provided vital air transport support to a nation at war. Everything was subject to the inevitable vagaries and restrictions of wartime conditions, and forward planning for peacetime civilian operation was, at best, uncertain. One of the corporation's first moves when the war ended in 1945 was to set up a Design Committee and appoint a design consultant, Kenneth Holmes. They were given the challenging task of 'harmonising the manifold activities of BOAC into a characteristic 'style' which will be representative of the best British design and workmanship , and which will create prestige both for the corporation and Great Britain throughout the world.'[83]

Two years later, Holmes set out his stall in a special issue of *Art & Industry* magazine, which was entirely devoted to BOAC. He began with a homage to Frank Pick and his design achievements before the war at London Transport, which were already seen as the benchmark for public corporations. In the optimistic spirit of the 'Britain Can Make It' exhibition held at the Victoria and Albert Museum in 1946, which prefigured the confident underlining of design's role in Britain's post-war industrial recovery so evident at the Festival of Britain in 1951, Holmes laid out BOAC's two-fold design mission. It was to 'employ good design as an agent to build goodwill by promoting interest in British production of goods as well as aircraft; in fact to harness art to the service of the community.' Secondly, the intention was to 'co-ordinate design throughout all activities undertaken by the Corporation, and to achieve by so doing a cumulative and therefore powerful effect'.

This was a formal articulation of corporate design policy that had never been made by Imperial Airways before the war. Despite the inevitable difficulties of post-war shortages and concerns

86 Make do and mend.
BOAC female cabin crew in wartime military-style uniforms c.1945. The aircraft is one of the 60 rugged Douglas Dakota C47 transport planes supplied by the Americans that sustained BOAC operations after 1943.

The Speedbird symbol had been retained throughout the war, but every other aspect of design, from staff uniforms to aircraft, was about to be given a new look with the reinstatement of civilian services.

85 Fly to the Far East
Designer: Rowland Hilder
BOAC poster in association with QEA, SAA and TEAL, 1948

An image which encapsulates the transition period of British aviation just after the war. The location is Victoria Harbour, Hong Kong. The BOAC flying boat moored beyond the traditional Chinese craft is a Sandringham, the civilian conversion of the wartime Sunderland launched in November 1945. An American built Lockheed Constellation airliner soars overhead. These new landplanes, operated by BOAC in conjunction with Qantas Empire Airways, cut the long journey in stages from London to Sydney to just 4½ days compared to 10½ days by flying boat. BOAC sold off all its remaining flying boats in 1950.

Rowland Hilder (1905–93) is an interesting choice of artist for this poster. He was much better known for his pastoral watercolour views of the English countryside, particularly of Kent and produced book illustrations and posters for Shell, the main line railway companies and the Ministry of Information.

about how full nationalisation might be applied, BOAC's public commitment to high design standards as a core value of the whole organisation was quickly evident. The Speedbird logo inherited from Imperial now became more prominent than ever as the symbolic heart of British civil aviation, and the name became a synonym for the national airline in advertising and publicity campaigns. *Art & Industry* magazine helpfully provided a list of what they described, in a slightly sinister Orwellian phrase, as the 'designers and manufacturers who co-operated with the BOAC Design Committee'. It covers everything from badges, buttons and lunch boxes (Meriel Millel) to tailored women's uniforms (Helman of London) and from menus

and calendars (Susan Einzig and Victor Reinganum) to complete aircraft interior schemes (Richard Lonsdale-Hands and associates for the new Avro Tudor).

Suddenly it was important for every aspect of BOAC to reflect quality and good, tasteful British design standards, which were thought to be distinctively different from what many saw as the flashy, superficial styling of American consumer design. Ironically, several of the leading 'British' designers of this era were not British born at all but had come to work in Britain in the 1930s as refugees and émigrés from the sterile and threatening culture of the Nazis that was spreading across the Continent.

SPEEDBIRD

The B O A C Magazine Winter 1947

Some of them worked across the piece on posters, graphics, liveries, exhibitions and interiors, notably the Bauhaus-trained artist Beverly Pick (1916–96) and German-born designer F.H.K. Henrion (1914–90) who both combined stylish elements of European modernism with more traditional British design strands. This proved to be a very creative mix which was well represented at BOAC. Henrion was particularly influential on BOAC's 'new look', becoming art director for all publications in the late 1940s, including *Speedbird* magazine, the inevitably named BOAC post-war house journal.

Unfortunately the high quality publicity and impressive graphic design at BOAC in the late 1940s was not matched by decisive and consistent policy making in the more critical field of aircraft development and procurement. The Government, BOAC and the British aircraft industry between them failed to develop a realistic strategy for post-war civil aviation, despite the continuing political commitment to 'buy British' for the national airline.

In the absence of a suitable available domestic product, American Lockheed Constellation and Boeing Stratocruiser airliners were acquired for use on BOAC's long range Australian and transatlantic routes. Meanwhile British manufacturers wasted time and money on expensive development projects for large new pressurised all-metal airliners. There were two particularly notorious duds: the huge Bristol Brabazon landplane and the giant Saunders-Roe Princess flying boat. Each proved to be, for

different reasons, a complete white elephant and neither went into mass production or even entered passenger service.

In 1950, when BOAC was officially ten years old, the future of British civil aviation in an austere post-war country, where rationing was still in place, must have felt more about promise and potential than delivery. In January Lord Pakenham, the air minister, named the flagship of the new Stratocruiser fleet *Caledonia* at a ceremony at Prestwick airport, near Glasgow. This was intended to be a special tribute to Scotland but was also in memory of the pre-war Empire Flying Boats, of which *Caledonia* had been the first to make a transatlantic proving flight for Imperial Airways in 1937.

Transferring old flying boat names to the ten BOAC Stratocruisers was an appropriate gesture looking back to the recent past but also represented a significant transitional move forward. BOAC had just introduced a London–New York service via Prestwick with the luxurious new double-deck Stratocruisers.

In July, the minister was on hand again at the fast developing new London Airport (Heathrow) to resurrect the name *Hannibal,* given to Imperial's original HP42 in 1931, for the flagship of the new Handley Page Hermes fleet. This was the first British built post-war airliner to enter service with BOAC, and new Vickers Viscount turbo-props were also eagerly awaited by both BOAC and BEA. Before the year was out the last BOAC passenger flying boat service had left Southampton for South Africa, ending the reliance on flying boats as the core providers on the former Empire routes, now to be a modern landplane network linking the post-colonial countries of the Commonwealth. The management, operations, airports and aircraft of the national carrier no longer bore any resemblance to their pre-war incarnations.

Queen and Comet: Art and Aviation in the New Elizabethan Age

SCOTT ANTHONY

The Rebirth of British Civil Aviation

**105 BOAC Flies to All
6 continents**
Designer: Abram Games
BOAC poster, c.1956

**89 BEA BOAC BSAA –
British Airways**
Designer: G.R. Morris
BEA, BOAC, BSAA poster,
c.1946

A new Britain came into being in the 1950s. Victorious in war, the British had united to revamp the social order; prosperity and a future as a pre-eminent hi-tech nation awaited. Such was the mood crystallised by Queen Elizabeth II's ascension to the throne in 1952. 'Where the sixteenth century had Johnson, the twentieth had Christopher Fry,' as the *Daily Herald* had it, 'for Herrick they had Dylan Thomas, for Beaumont, Rattigan. Shakespeare remains unchallenged. In other fields, for Drake read any BOAC [British Overseas Airways Corporation] pilot.'[84]

'The New Elizabethan era' christened by Winston Churchill was to become an age of global media and global travel. The 1953 coronation demonstrated something of how these two trends became intertwined. The young Queen had grown up in the media spotlight. She was familiar to millions from a best-selling memoir about her childhood (*The Little Princesses*), from images of her changing the wheel of an Army truck as a teenager during the war and from a deluge of magazine features that focused on her life as a young mother. Because of the mass media, the nation heard of her

father's death on the BBC before she did, and then followed her progress on the 24-hour BOAC flight home from East Africa. As popular anticipation rose during the 16 months between Queen Elizabeth II's ascension to the throne and her coronation, there was a spike in the purchase of television sets: a very new kind of bond between the monarch and the masses was being forged. In the weeks ahead of the coronation millions of visitors arrived in London. The garlands of the New Elizabethan age were to be television and tourism.

Interest in the coronation went beyond Britain and the Commonwealth. A television link-up saw the event screened in France, the Netherlands and West Germany. The American news channel CBS converted a BOAC plane into a mobile film-editing studio, cutting its newsreels together in the sky ready for instant distribution when the plane touched down in the United States. The American financier Bernard Baruch dubbed Queen Elizabeth II 'the world's sweetheart'. One observer compared the coronation's gathering of extras – from bishops, sheiks and sultans to generals and tribesmen – to a Hollywood epic. BOAC and British European

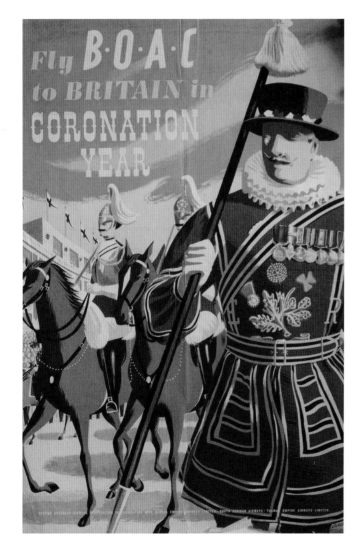

**91 Fly BOAC to Britain
in Coronation Year**
Designer: Adelman
BOAC poster, c.1953

**92 Vôe a Grã-Bretana
Pela BOAC**
Unknown designer
BOAC poster, c.1953

Here is an aeroplane of beauty—the new BEA Elizabethan. Its spacious, comfortable cabin has huge windows, giving you a wonderful view of sky and landscape beneath the high-set wing. The all-British Airspeed Elizabethan is pressurized to fly at fine-weather heights; cruising at nearly five miles a minute, it can cut flying time to Paris by a quarter.

BRITISH EUROPEAN AIRWAYS

Airways (BEA) had played a major role in ferrying this international cast to London. Flowers and gifts arrived via BOAC from Bombay, Colombo, Karachi, Johannesburg, Salisbury, Sydney, Kingston and Dar es Salaam. BEA had renamed the new Airspeed Ambassador aircraft 'the Elizabethan' and resurrected Imperial Airways' luxury 'Silver Wing' service to Paris to serve VIPs. 'The Coronation was like a phoenix-time,' remembered Princess Margaret, 'everything was being raised from the ashes. There was this gorgeous looking, lovely young lady, and nothing to stop everything getting better and better.'[85]

As a prompt of technological innovation, as a tool of global diplomacy and as a boost to British trade, the British Overseas Airways Corporation was fated to play an important role in the brave new post-war world. It was charged with consolidating native expertise in manufacturing, design and organisation to ensure Britain kept pace with rival superpowers, the United States and the USSR. Although BOAC had officially come into being on 1 April 1940, civil aviation had been curtailed by war and the corporation resurrected by the Air Corporations Act of 1946 was driven by both a hungry-eyed ambition and a determination to fend off American supremacy. Civil aviation was given three immediate priorities: the restarting of long-haul Empire routes, the consolidation of short-haul European routes (undertaken by BEA) and the establishment of a short-lived South American subsidiary (British South American Airways [BSAA]). This was a political attempt to jump start the civil aviation industry that had been abandoned in 1939. The expertise that had enabled the nation to prevail in the Battle of Britain was to be retooled to ensure Britain retained its status as a global air power in peacetime.

New Elizabethan ambitions made BOAC into the national flag-carrying airline in the broadest sense. Early publicity emphasised its role in alleviating famines and flooding, in the supply of medicines and in the transportation of athletes and explorers. More than this, BOAC strove to embed itself in the cultural fabric of the nation. By taking pressurised oxygen canisters to climbers on Everest, transporting a 7,000 year-old skull from the British School in Jerusalem or flying astronomers as close as possible to an eclipse over the Shetland Islands, BOAC presented itself as a national service aware of its wider responsibilities. Like many of the corporations formed during the inter-war period,

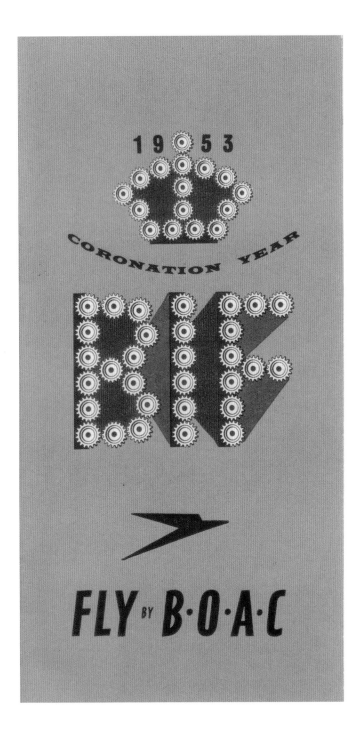

such as the BBC, ICI and London Transport,
BOAC adopted an expansive managerial ethos
informed by the social effects of the slump. In 1945
no firm wanted to be accused of being staffed by
hard-faced men who had done well out of the war.
Of course, the fact that no large passenger market
existed meant that BOAC's cultural interventions
could also be rationalised as the long-term building
of a brand. New Elizabethan ambitions fermented
in a culture where the pursuit of profit was balanced
against the demands of national prestige; when these
values shifted later in the post-war period so did
BOAC's public mode of address.

The appointment of Miles Thomas (1897–1980)
as Chairman in 1949 was to be crucial to BOAC's
success. Thomas had been recruited from Lord
Nuffield's motor empire (which included Morris)
with the instruction ruthlessly to ready British
civil aviation for the post-war challenges ahead.
The Labour government wanted Thomas to do
for BOAC what Lord Ashfield had done for London
Transport during the inter-war period – mould
a disparate organisation into an efficient whole.[86]
The first challenge was to integrate the South
American routes of BSAA, which had been unable
to break into a market long-dominated by North
American carriers, and was quickly submerged
into BOAC. Under Thomas the firm's enthusiastic
forays into frozen food, plastic manufacture and
the building of aircraft weighing machines would
be similarly curtailed.

Thomas began his reign by dispensing with some
84 executives; a further third of the entire staff,
some 7,000 people, followed them out of the door.
Next, he grappled with the begged and borrowed
aspect of BOAC's post-war fleet; it flew 17 types
of planes powered by 16 different kinds of engines.
Thomas' task was gradually to ease converted
military planes out of service and streamline the

fleet. This streamlining in turn allowed the number of maintenance bases to be reduced from eight to two. The flying boats that had been a staple of Imperial's pre-war fleet were finally retired in 1950. Three years into Thomas's reign, BOAC turned its first profit. The immediate goal might have been consolidation, but the longer term aim was far more ambitious. The company had invested in a revolutionary jet-engine plane that would transform air travel forever. The post-war strategy of BOAC entailed waiting for this long-bet to pay out.

In the early posters of BOAC and BEA the exotic destinations were printed in a matter-of-fact typeface that looked like it had been borrowed from the front of a London bus. This was no coincidence. One of the most important managerial ideas BOAC appropriated from London Transport was an engagement with publicity and industrial design. Modern corporations such as the General Post Office, the BBC, Shell, ICI and Unilever had led the development of public relations in the 1930s. Quality was the watchword of these inter-war media interventions, as corporate business responded to the cultural and political pressures of the economic slump by broadly aligning itself with social and educational progress.

As the nation's chosen instrument for the development of a key industry, BOAC would continue to sponsor museum exhibitions and commission challenging public artworks during the early post-war period. 'The Corporation's policy is founded in good traditions of design,' as the corporation had it, 'it's a policy that has already brought its reward; not only in the commercial sense, but from the point of view of prestige and morale.'[87] However, the accent of this policy was already beginning to shift. As the 1950s progressed the separation between 'sales' and 'publicity' that had been a hallmark of Imperial Airways (and corporate publicity as practised during the inter-war period as a whole) would be further dissolved. Although BOAC was to maintain its commitment to quality – from Staffordshire pottery to beech and oak furniture designed by Frank Chippindale – their choices were increasingly made with an eye on a more economically motivated definition of national interest. Aviation was an important dollar earner for an austerity-plagued Britain, bringing businessmen and tourists to the country. One of BOAC's jobs was to provide a window for modern British goods. The BOAC posters of this period advertise Gauge & Tool exhibitions, agricultural shows and international trade fairs from Brussels to Baghdad.

Although BOAC worked with advertising agencies such as Colman, Prentis and Varley, it built up its own group of internal expertise. Recruited from the RAF, the company's first publicity team tended to fall back on visual idioms that had been developed by artists working for the Ministry of Information during the war. Their public relations strategy focused on advertising new aircraft, raising awareness of the company's routes and building the BOAC brand. The form this advertising took tended to reflect the enthusiasms of the publicity staff. Particularly influential was company photographer Henry Hensser, who joined the company after making his name as a war photographer. In the inter-war period there had been a modernist vogue for machine photography that used out-of-scale industrial objects to surrealistic effect, but Hensser wanted to more straightforwardly capture the ambition and aesthetic beauty of BOAC's engineering achievements.[88]

During this early post-war period it was the practicality of modern design that was most emphasised. The adoption of BOAC's blue and white livery was not just about looking pretty; it helped reflect short-wave solar radiation

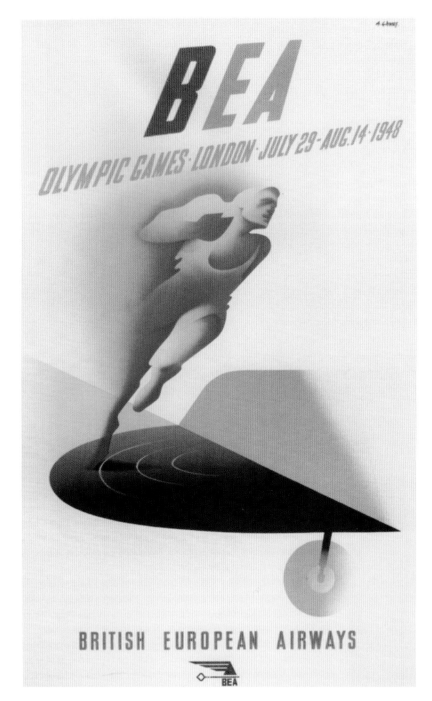

(or 'Latest Livery Means Cooler Customers',
as the headline put it) and made their planes
easier to clean.[88] Other engineering innovations
would prompt BOAC to become a key patron
of modernism in Britain. BOAC's enormous, 250
metre-long maintenance headquarters at London
Airport (now Heathrow), completed in 1952,
boasted the longest reinforced concrete spans in
the world. Designed by Sir Owen Williams, it
placed London Airport in a lineage of state-of-the-
art construction that stretched from the Wembley
Exhibition of 1924 to the contemporaneous
development of a motorway network. This was
British empiricists doing continental avant-garde.

**99 Olympic Games –
Frequent Services by
Comfortable BOAC
Landplanes & Flying Boats**
Original artwork: Walter Herz
BOAC poster, 1947–8

The British national airlines
used their posters to try and
connect the internationalist
spirit of the Olympic Games
with the development of mass
transport systems and tourism.
Abram Games (who earned
the nickname 'Olympic Games'
by designing the London 1948
stamps) designed a poster for
BEA, transforming the image
of a nose cone of a plane into
a running track. Walter Herz,
meanwhile, superimposed
an image of Discobolus from
the British Museum on to the
Houses of Parliament. This
general approach was repeated
at the subsequent Helsinki
Games of 1952, although
by then cold war rivalries were
beginning to encroach on to
the sports field.

100 BOAC – It's a Small World by Speedbird
Designer: F.H.K. Henrion
BOAC poster, 1947

it's a small world by Speedbird

BRITISH OVERSEAS AIRWAYS CORPORATION IN ASSOCIATION WITH QANTAS EMPIRE AIRWAYS · SOUTH AFRICAN AIRWAYS AND TASMAN EMPIRE AIRWAYS LIMITED

101 It's a Smaller World by Speedbird – fly BOAC
Designer: Beverley Pick
BOAC poster, 1948

Abram Games and the Festival of Britain

Perhaps the most extraordinary individual artist involved in the creation of BOAC's post-war image was Abram Games (1914–96). The 'Fly the Atlantic by BOAC' poster shows something of Games at his best. The poster depicts Speedbird tearing through an old map. It's a striking, exciting image which, beyond giving an impression of rapidity, also communicates the idea that BOAC has wrenched the two nations closer together. Against this, there's an air of deliberateness and poise about the poster. The accelerative rush of the image is kept in check by the strict balance of its composition. Its BOAC commissioners were delighted by the poster's visceral and psychological impact.

Born in 1914 Games was part of a generation of artists that had inadvertently developed what came to be known as 'graphic design'.[90] Influenced by European modernism, in particular the posters of Lucian Bernhard and Julius Klinger in Germany, Cassandre and Paul Colin in France, and Edward McKnight Kauffer in Britain, Games had picked up commissions through the progressive advertising agency Crawfords during the 1930s. He balanced prestige work for companies such as Shell with

'belief' projects for organisations such as the Royal Society for the Protection of Accidents. In common with many of his peers he saw himself as working in public information rather than advertising. Poster design, in this formation, operated as a cultural middleman between great scientific and social change and life as it was lived on a day-to-day level. Games' work trusted that relatively small gestures in design would eventually have larger cumulative consequences. 'An idea has to be implanted in the audience,' he wrote, 'but it has to be implanted imaginatively, in such a way as to fire the interest and kindle a response to new thinking.'[91]

By designing the Festival of Britain logo (and a set of commemorative stamps) Games became inextricably associated with the brightest ambitions of post-war Britain. The 1951 Festival had sought to self-consciously emulate the Great Exhibition of 1851, aiming to be both a celebration of the national character and a demonstration of Britain's continuing artistic, cultural and scientific pre-eminence.[92] Radars and efficient factory layouts were exhibited alongside modern British artists and indigenous arcana such as the Tempest

102 Fly the Atlantic by BOAC
Designer: Abram Games
BOAC poster, c.1951

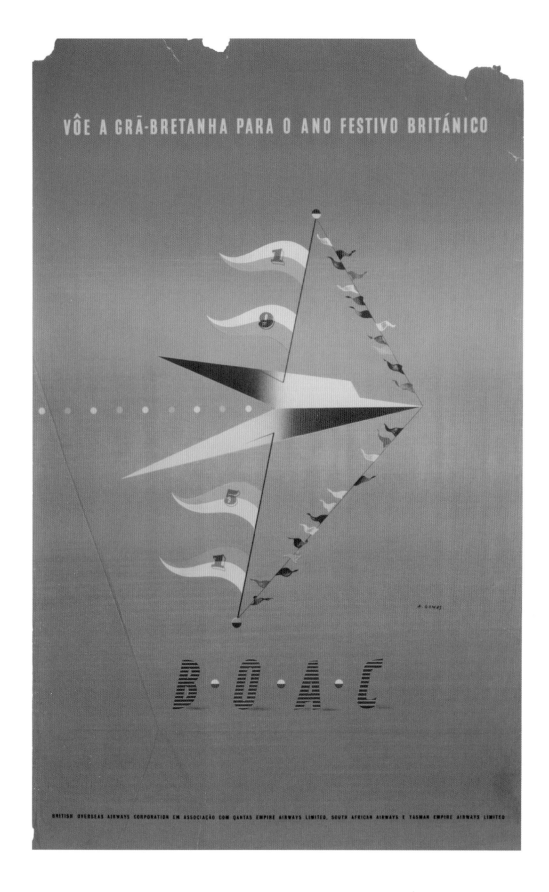

103 Vôe a Grã-Bretana
para o ano Festivo
Británico BOAC
Designer: Abram Games
BOAC poster, c.1951

Prognosticator in an effort to educate popular taste and encourage technical enthusiasms. Following his work on the Festival, Games produced the logo for BBC television (he also worked extensively for Murphy Televisions) as well as iconic work for BEA and BOAC. Thus the spartan logo Games produced for the Festival came, for a time, to operate as a sort of visual shorthand for all that was modern in Britain, and Games himself became the British designer of choice for the maturing new industries of the mid-twentieth century.

The Festival of Britain gave the population a brief glimpse of what the future might look like. It illustrated how modern technology might alter the way in which the nation lived. But the Festival was also materially important to civil aviation at a more mundane level. The Ministry of Supply that had helped construct the Festival remained responsible for the construction of the new national airlines' facilities and in 1953 BEA seized the opportunity to open its new departure terminal on part of the old Festival site. 'The Festival of Britain brought a new spirit into British architecture and design and this was at once apparent to the thousands of visitors who emerged from the nether regions via the Underground and entered the grounds through the gay and ultra-modern Station Gate,' BEA boasted. 'It seems fitting that the same building, adapted to our needs, should become the Town Terminal of Britain's youngest and most enterprising Air Corporation.'[93] BEA's striking terminal at London's Waterloo station (where passengers checked-in) provided a provocative contrast with the prefabs and caravans that met travellers on arrival at London Airport.

A decade into the post-war period, Games had become an internationally renowned figure. In lectures across the world he stressed the importance of designers maintaining their independence as

'middlemen'. Games' posters may frequently have been humorous, but he invariably hoped to make a serious point. Using a favoured anthropomorphic technique, his poster for BEA cargo saw two propeller engines transform into giant hands, while a poster promoting business travel showed a wing becoming a pinstriped arm carrying a briefcase. 'My work has been called symbolic,' said Games, 'but I regard it as integration, a combination of all the parts in to an inevitable whole.' He continued, 'In the same way a man and newspaper are everyday sights, integrated by design the unit becomes a "mannewspaper" as it were, an entirely new object demanding closer study. This visual shorthand has been developed over the years into a language of expression for me. I have tried to use it to express thoughts on subjects from culture and commerce.'[94] Design was not 'mere salesmanship' to Games.

Games believed that good design could play a part in the wider improvement of society. This was a belief cemented by the experience of the Second World War. Producing posters for the Ministry of Information brought into harness, in Games' opinion, an enlightened patron, a worthwhile project and the best instincts of an audience. At the Ministry of Information, Games had also been among the first to see pictures of concentration camps in Nazi Germany, an experience which further deepened his conviction about the absolute importance of maintaining a kind of everyday integrity as well as securing his support for the creation of the state of Israel. But while improvements in design during the Second World War had been driven by a series of nationally unifying factors, Games believed a dawning age of internationalism, underpinned by the universal nature of consumer products such as motor cars and washing machines, would drive a similarly exceptional pan-national advance in

post-war design. He hoped that this emerging new visual vocabulary could help build an international community able to withstand the apocalyptic pressures of the atomic age. This sounds loftily idealistic, but it indicates something of the seriousness and sincerity with which Games selected his briefs. Aviation was important to Games partly because he believed it was fundamentally an internationalist technology.

The 1960s saw a step-change in the character of Games' work that was to be reflected in his later designs for BOAC. Posters such as 'USA – Fly BOAC', which transformed two BOAC tailfins

107 British European Airways to British Industries Fair
Designer: Abram Games
BEA poster, c.1951

108 Fly Freight BEA
Designer: Abram Games
BEA poster, c.1954

109 BEA built their new
Waterloo terminal on the old
Festival of Britain site, c.1953.

and the top of a skyscraper into a Stetson hat, were
illustrative of Games' effort to break out of the
controlled, often static work with which he had
made his name. Games' ethos had been 'maximum
meaning, minimum means', but his posters began
to turn instead to looser forms, pulsing with strong
colours. This freer approach perhaps reflected the
rise of Abstract Expressionism, but it was also true
that Games' work was changing with the nature
of his commissions. A mass consumer culture was
emerging, the business of advertising was becoming
more specialised and the visual idioms employed
were becoming ever more aggressive. Clarity
was being outshone by bold new styles. 'Not for
nothing has the broad grin become advertising's
most universal symbol in post-war years,' remarked
a disapproving Games. 'Most international posters
have in one way or another provided the circus
atmosphere, reflecting the constant and wild search
for entertainment to escape from the realities of
our lives.'[95]

In an environment that drew ever more on the
insights of psychological research, Games' restraint
and dislike of 'methods which are not wholesome'
began to fall out of fashion. In later years, Games
would become more associated with stately prestige
projects or public information campaigns (for
example, Games employed an image of Britannia

as a street sweeper for the drive to 'Keep Britain
Tidy') especially for issues related to displaced
persons or Jewish causes. However, Games
also continued to work closely with Freeman's
Catalogue, Horizon holidays, El Al Israel Airlines
and for Israeli tourist organisations. For better or
worse, the bright and breezy manner of Games'
later BOAC posters sensed their way towards an
emerging culture of glossy brochures and package
holidays to the Mediterranean.

110 On Business Fly BEA
Designer: Abram Games
BEA poster, c.1954

111 Greetings – BEA
Designer: Abram Games
BEA poster, c.1958

Flying Across the Commonwealth

In one of the most memorable images produced for the coronation, the Queen's sceptre doubles as a globe around which the various peoples of the Commonwealth orbit. If building Empire communications had been the raison d'être of pre-war British civil aviation, BOAC found itself having to adapt to the new reality of the Commonwealth as a multicultural association of independent states. In the immediate aftermath of the coronation little appeared to have changed as Queen Elizabeth II embarked on a five-and-a-half month flying tour of the Commonwealth that took in Australia, New Zealand, Bermuda, Jamaica, Fiji, Tonga, the Coco Islands, Aden, Uganda, Malta and Gibraltar. Yet as the process of decolonisation accelerated, BOAC began to play a different kind of role. A little paradoxically, preparations for the independence of British colonies in Asia and Africa necessitated the huge expansion of the Colonial Office during the early post-war period. The training of administrators, statisticians and scientists thought necessary for the successful transition of power required ever closer communications with Britain. One unusual marker of this was the large increase in the number of children carried by BOAC. By 1957 BOAC's Junior Jet Club had more than 1,500 members. If nothing else, the expansion of the Colonial Service increased the number of public schoolboys commuting back and forth to Britain.

Just as imperial priorities led Imperial Airways to underwrite the establishment of companies such as QANTAS and Indian Trans-Continental, BOAC subsidised 'partner' airlines, such as those in Aden, Central Africa, Cyprus, East Africa, the Gulf, Hong Kong, Taiwan and the West Indies, in the name of decolonisation. Hence posters advertising BOAC routes often overlaid previous work done by Imperial Airways. The Empire route maps of the pre-war age remained a standard motif of BOAC's posters, albeit they now tended to be given a harder, geometric treatment in keeping with both the visual rhetoric of the atomic age and the popularity of crystal structure designs made fashionable by the Festival of Britain. There is perhaps an analogy to be drawn here between the hardy services performed by BOAC and the success of its British 4x4 contemporary, the Land Rover. Both were modern technological instruments

112 Africa – Fly There by BOAC
Designer: Eric Pulford
BOAC poster, c.1959

113 Save $ – Malayan Airways Ltd
Designer: Papineau
Malayan Airways poster,
c.1954

114 To Nairobi by BOAC and then East African Airways to All Parts of East Africa
Unknown designer
BOAC poster in association with
East African Airways, c.1960

BOAC's relationship with its feeder airlines became an important part of the 'constructive decolonisation' programme instigated by the post-war Labour administration. Indian National Airways is now part of Air India, BWIA has become Caribbean Airlines, Malayan Airlines would split into Malaysian Airlines and Singapore Airlines, while East African Airways spun off into Kenya Airways, Air Tanzania and (the now defunct) Air Uganda in 1977.

of a serious purpose – helping to supervise irrigation schemes, conduct geological surveys and establish universities. Or at least that was the image they projected.

BOAC's investments were both far-sightedly beneficent and calculatedly strategic. Civil aviation was a loss-making high-tech industry and BOAC's input into the building of a new airport in Dar es Salaam, for instance, was thought to help reinforce and renew existing commercial, social and political relationships with Britain, even as overall political responsibility passed from London. On the one hand, BOAC pilots and administrators were involved with the higher education and training of aviation staff in Nigeria and the Gold Coast

(now Ghana) as part of the 'Africanisation' of West African Airways. On the other hand, the tours British planes made of the Commonwealth were about securing sales. Thus, in one month in 1951 Sir Frank Whittle (1907–96), inventor of the jet engine and BOAC ambassador, had audiences with the Shah, the King of Iraq, the President of Lebanon and the Sheiks of Bahrain and Kuwait in order to help promote the de Havilland Comet. To an extent it was a successful strategy. Experienced in producing planes for extremes of temperature (and basic airfields), British aircraft manufacturers were well placed to retain orders. Firms such as Rolls-Royce are arguably still benefiting from this hard-won experience today.

**115 Indian National Airways
– Fly Indiaman**
Designer: Amar
Indian National Airways poster,
c.1948

**116 Jamaica British West
Indies – Fly by BOAC
and BWIA**
Unknown designer
BOAC poster in association
with BWIA, c.1955

The consequence, however, was perhaps to skew British manufacturing priorities away from being able to compete in the American market, which was to dominate much of the post-war period. It was more than an accident of geography that British aircraft manufacturers excelled in the development of short- and medium-haul planes rather than the longer-range efforts of American manufacturers.

BOAC played an interesting role in the new diplomacy of Commonwealth. The British monarch's sovereign powers over 'dominions' had been replaced by a personal link, in which the monarch established a unique relationship with each country of the Commonwealth as the 'King of the British Dominions beyond the Seas' became

117 (top left) BOAC Hermes, Kano, c.1951.
The schoolchildren of colonial administrators were important BOAC customers.

118 (top right) BOAC attempted to woo liner passengers by erecting hoardings along the Suez canal, c.1951

119 (bottom) BOAC Comet 4 advert, Khartoum, c.1958. Aviation expertise was to help Britain maintain links with former colonies.

'Queen of her other Realms and Territories'. In this context it made sense that BOAC increasingly made a noisy virtue of the fact that it served political leaders and administrators such as Sayed Ismail El Azhari (Sudan), Michael Okorodudu (Nigeria) and Haile Selassie (Ethiopia). BOAC made substantial charitable donations, awarding scholarships to British universities for newly independent nations such as Malaya, and was also proactive in recruiting (and promoting) local staff. In 1958, for an illustrative example, it became the first airline to employ Indian and Pakistani stewardesses, who adopted a green with gold trim sari as their uniform. Such touches illustrate how the company shifted to a softer diplomacy, partly in an effort to protect pre-existing routes and commercial relationships.

Altogether less coy was BOAC's promotion of what had once been the white dominions of the British Empire. 'Fly High, Play Low' read one BOAC hoarding that promised 'a swinging time in Sydney'. The photograph shows a stripper throwing off her clothes. It is unlikely that such an image would have been used to promote flights in Africa or Asia. As well as arguably marking a newfound civility towards the former colonies, the vigorous images of life in Australia, Canada and New Zealand were calculated to appeal to the desires of British emigrants. The working relationship first established between Imperial Airways and QANTAS Empire Airways in the inter-war period prospered anew as Australia was aggressively promoted as a land of sun, sea and opportunity.

120 Australia – Fly There by BOAC and QANTAS
Designer: Hayes
BOAC poster in association
with QANTAS, c.1956

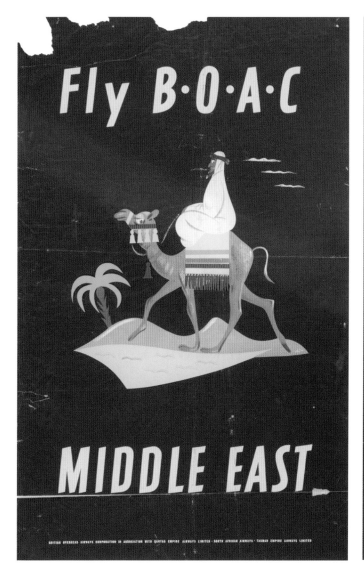

122 Fly BOAC – Middle East
Designer: Aldo Cosomati
BOAC poster, c.1958

123 Fly BOAC – Pakistan
Designer: Aldo Cosomati
BOAC poster, c.1958

The Art of Flight: Serving Passengers and Staff

At the turn of the 1950s every ninth passenger on BOAC was an animal. The company's role in the supply of polo horses, the treatment of sick animals from Africa or the delivery of pandas to London Zoo became a mainstay of BOAC's positive appearances in the media. 'Crocodiles don't need feeding for up to six days but must be hosed daily,' as one BOAC staff member explained, 'while anthropoid apes – need blankets and company if not by an ape then a human. Monkeys can be taught to queue.'[96] In a series of posters by Aldo Cosomati (1895–1977), countries are reduced to a representative animal; the Middle East is a camel, Pakistan is a tiger and Switzerland a cow. The posters work in the same idiom as Cosomati's work for the Underground in the 1920s (where his use of simple bright designs had been used to promote Hampton Court Palace, the Richmond horse show and the north London suburb of Barnet) but it's interesting to ponder whether the popularity of such iconography among BOAC management also reflected something of the reality of day-to-day operations at the airline. Not only did the airline carry some 30,000 animal passengers a year, but

for a time there even appears to have been a fashion for BOAC crews to keep parrots on the flight deck. Of course, as the post-war period progressed and flying became ever more affordable, the image of the airline and its passengers changed radically.

The coronation had done a great deal for the status, reputation and visibility of BOAC's operations and the service the company provided to the British royal family remained an important part of its public image. As the 1950s wore on, however, the patronage of the American film industry also became important. BOAC boasted that it carried stars such as Jack Benny, Elizabeth Taylor, Katherine Hepburn and Douglas Fairbanks Jr, as well as stage actors such as Rex Harrison, Laurence Olivier, Vivien Leigh and John Gielgud. Indeed, the professional diversity of the wealthy passengers BOAC carried, from opera singers to stars of popular musicals, from international plutocrats to celebrated plastic surgeons like Archibald McIndoe, was central to the appeal of aviation. The posters and press materials of this period show how BOAC's public image slowly shifted from emphasising national prestige to its role

124 We Are Proud of Our Fleet at BEA
Unknown designer
BEA poster, c.1953

We are proud of our air fleet at

BRITISH EUROPEAN AIRWAYS

FINEST AIR FLEET IN EUROPE

126 BEA and BOAC both emphasised their role in transporting rare and sick animals, c.1966

127 BOAC – No Tips Please
Unknown designer
BOAC sign, c.1952

in linking Britain with the wider world and then to selling tickets to an ever-widening public. BOAC posters were moving away from more abstract styles to become mini-brochures. Increasingly BOAC advertising concentrated on reassuring potential customers by showing them the pilots that flew you, the staff that served you and the cabin you flew in.

One of the most striking aspects of BOAC's managerial practices was its distinctive culture. A key personality behind this was Sir Basil Smallpeice (1906–92), who would succeed Miles Thomas as Chairman in 1956. Smallpeice, perhaps because he was an outsider in the rather closed world of aviation, shared the rude facts and figures of the company's performance with staff in an effort to encourage their initiative and reward loyalty. One of the successes of BOAC's early poster campaigns was a series starring 'real' workers produced for the Festival of Britain.

As it was an open secret that BOAC did not have the best planes it was entirely rational that the company made a virtue out of its people, but the respect from the managerial ranks downwards was built upon more than the pragmatics of promoting the company to the public. Many BOAC staff had been in aviation from its experimental beginnings – starting their 'careers' as wing-walkers or in display teams. BOAC pilots were veterans of hundreds of transatlantic flights made in wartime to deliver American supplies to the Allies. The standards of safety and airmanship established during the war were something of which the company remained justifiably proud. The norms of the company might have been formal, and symbolised by the stiff, tailored suits of the employees, but the spirit of camaraderie appeared genuine. Subsidised housing was rapidly constructed in Staines, Stanwell and Hounslow to accommodate maintenance workers moved south from Scotland at the end of the

war. The building of a staff club in Brentford was a concession towards the new era of industrial relations supposedly ushered in by the election of Clement Attlee's reforming Labour government in 1945, but it also reflected a collective ethos inherited from wartime experience.

As the post-war period progressed these holistic strengths would be more ambivalently assessed. As the demands of a consumer market began to make themselves heard the enthusiasm and simple reverence for flying that characterised BOAC's manner began to acquire more negative connotations. As the post-war era stretched on BOAC's apparent gruffness could be mistaken for condescension. Asked, 'How would you describe Sharjah?' a BOAC press officer replied, 'Ruddy awful.'[97] Smallpeice and many of BOAC's staff came from an era when British civil aviation thought of itself as a family. In the future a rising generation of politicians tended to dismiss the organisation and its war-era values as remote from everyday concerns and out-of-touch with the realities of the business world.

The Coming of the Comet

On 6 September 1946, a jet-powered RAF Meteor hit 616.81 mph (992.66 km/h) to break the world airspeed record. Below, crowds had massed on the beaches and coastal paths between Bognor Regis and Worthing to witness history in the making. The pilot of the record-breaking Meteor, Group Captain E.M. Donaldson, flew without a helmet and plugged his ears with gun-cotton. 'That's all for today,' he told the jubilant crowd, 'now I must see mother.'[98] The nation was hooked. If the daring and pluck of Spitfire pilots had fired a thousand *Boy's Own* dreams during the Second World War, then in the immediate post-war period it was the exploits of Donaldson and other British test pilots (men and women) that excited the imagination as they pushed ever closer to breaking the sound barrier.[99]

It is commonplace to note that wars are bonfires for old technologies, and their conclusions trailers for new technologies and new cultures. Although Frank Whittle had conceived of jet propulsion in 1929, it was not until the production of Nazi jet aircraft that his ideas were systematically pursued in Britain. In 1944, as part of a far-reaching effort to ready the nation for peace, a British government committee sought to prompt the country's manufacturers into developing a jet airliner suitable for post-war civilian use. If jets were to be the future of air travel then Britain must lead the way. BOAC was ordered to buy 25 of what would eventually become the de Havilland Comet.

When it eventually entered service in 1952, Comet 1 caused a worldwide sensation. In a Pathé newsreel, a journalist on the inaugural BOAC flight to Johannesburg declares that the journey 'was so swift that you don't have time to get bored'.[100] That is quite a statement. London to Johannesburg on the Comet was a 23-hour flight that required six stops (Rome, Beirut, Cairo, Khartoum, Entebbe and Livingstone). In Khartoum there was an extra delay while the plane's interiors, as a standard practice of the day, were sprayed with insecticide. Of course, while the journalist's reaction seems extraordinary today, it's worth remembering that, pre-Comet, London to Johannesburg had taken more than 90 hours.

Comet 1 was celebrated as a triumph for de Havilland, whose order books quickly filled up, and a triumph for Miles Thomas. As a veteran

**128 BOAC Comet Jetliner –
Hasten at Leisure**
Designer: Kenneth Bromfield
BOAC poster, *c.*1952

of the car industry, Thomas had understood the importance of the embryonic Comet from the start. Aircraft, like automobiles, were the supreme mediators of the passenger experience, or to put it another way, in the days before aircraft manufacturing came to be dominated by Airbus and Boeing, a company's fleet defined its public image. The Comet had a cruising speed of 500 mph (805 km/h), twice the speed of its contemporary rivals. This was at a time when the rapid increases in the speed, size and altitude at which aircraft flew were some of the markers of post-war progress. As international orders flooded in, the Comet became the plane that epitomised the lead British scientists and manufacturers held over the rest of the world. The Comet seemed to illustrate both how quickly Britain had recovered from the exertions of the war and the nation's continuing pre-eminence as a global power. It was a plane designed to impress the neighbours, a national statement of intent. The Comet might even have been the greatest British artwork of the 1940s. 'It caused the American housewife to choose English china,' as one report gushed, 'her husband to buy a Jaguar automobile, and her son asked Santa Claus for a Raleigh bicycle for Christmas.'[101]

In sheer aesthetic terms, the Comet delivered. With its engines sculpted into the wings it was perhaps the most beautiful plane ever produced and quickly sidled its way alongside matinee stars, test cricketers and war heroes in popular affections. The Comet became a cocktail in fashionable West London hotels, starred in a Japanese film and was given a lyrical cameo in David Lean's *The Sound Barrier*. Interestingly, though, the Comet posters tend to be much more muted. The plane was assertively angular, stark and lean, but the posters advertising it frequently deployed humour and featured images of softly lit cabins

and families playing cards. Instructional cutaways and hazy, rather romantic sketches were also frequently employed. It's pertinent to note that the later Concorde was originally decorated in the muted tones of a Pall Mall gentleman's club (after privatisation, Concorde was refitted so that its seats resembled those of a high-end sports car) because British Airways did not want to frighten passengers with the thought of supersonic travel. Such thinking appears to have originated with the equally revolutionary Comet.

In May 1953, exactly one year after the Comet's introduction, one of the fleet broke up in a violent storm just after leaving Calcutta. Eight months later, a second Comet fell out of the sky over Italy. Two months after that, another plane suffered the same fate. The Royal Navy was ordered to retrieve

129 BOAC Comet 1 in Tokyo, c.1953. The futuristic form of the Comet featured in a film by celebrated Japanese director Tomo Uchida.

the wreckage from the sea. The RAF scientific establishment set to work on the causes of the accidents. The *Express* headline had been 'sabotage probe'[102] and popular belief in the Comet did not waver, but 9,000 hours of further testing revealed that its airframe was unable to withstand the rapid changes in altitude and pressure caused by jet propulsion. The Comet 1 was withdrawn. The de Havilland plane had been almost too far ahead of its time. BOAC's pioneering of the Comet immeasurably advanced the technology of civil aviation but plunged the company into debt and political disrepute.

In 1941, one of Frank Whittle's jet engines was unloaded at Bolling Field, Washington, DC. Its arrival prompted the Americans to launch a sustained programme of research in an area they had previously neglected. Bolstered by a long-haul domestic aviation market served by a number of competing carriers, US manufacturers began to develop their own jet planes. A prototype Boeing 707 was wheeled out in Seattle, Washington, just over a month after the final Comet 1 disaster. This remarkable plane, with a capacity of 140 (the first Comets could seat just 36 passengers), was to inaugurate the jumbo jet age and dominate civil aviation for the next decade. In 1958, de Havilland launched a successor, Comet 4, that would become the first jet to carry fare-paying passengers across the Atlantic, but it was not able to compete with the economies of scale offered by Boeing or the 707's greater range. So much had been invested in the Comet, financially and psychologically, that this fruitless achievement only exacerbated the sense of disappointment. People had lost their lives. Miles Thomas was broken by the failure. Comet 4 was obsolete within six years. One of the New Elizabethan age's grandest dreams had been rudely shaken.

130 The inaugural BOAC Comet 4 flight from London Heathrow to John F. Kennedy airport, New York, 1958.

(overleaf) **131 The Finest Then ... The Best Today – BOAC Takes Good Care of You**
Unknown designer
BOAC poster, c.1952

(overleaf) **132 BOAC Comet Jetliner – Lack of Vibration Reduces Travel Fatigue**
Unknown designer
BOAC poster, c.1952

Armstrong Whitworth Argosy

G-EBLF

The finest then...

...the best today

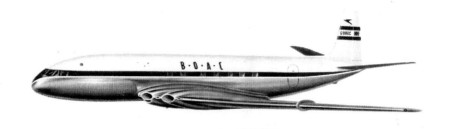

de Havilland Comet Jetliner

B·O·A·C TAKES GOOD CARE OF YOU
BRITISH OVERSEAS AIRWAYS CORPORATION

B·O·A·C *Comet* JETLINER

LACK OF VIBRATION REDUCES TRAVEL FATIGUE

BRITISH OVERSEAS AIRWAYS CORPORATION

51/508/13%/J.R.

The Rise of British European Airways

In September 1955 Gibbs toothpaste won the right, ahead of Guinness, Surf washing powder and Brown & Polson custard, to become the first product advertised on British television. Television, like aviation, had been one of the boom industries of the post-war period. Indeed, the impact of the BEA advert screened in February 1957 illustrated just how far the expansion of the two technologies had become intertwined. BEA's decision to advertise on commercial television was a move that prefigured a broader change of strategy. 'We are to concentrate,' as the company magazine had it, 'on CD1 – lower middle and upper working groups, instead of business men and wealthy people who go skiing or to the Continent.'[103] In 1948, BEA had just 24 marketing stands for display in the windows of travel agents; by the time the television advert aired it had 2,700. Bolstered by advertisements promising 'the holiday of your life', the TV campaign proved a strikingly successful promotion. 'The attractive young lady gambolling in the sea on posters and hoardings all over the country,' BEA's chairman wrote approvingly, 'has bought a sudden burst of Summer to the English Winter.'[104] Advertising the appeal of the Mediterranean sun in the north European gloom was certainly shrewd, and by allowing passengers to pay for their tickets by instalments, the company began to address some of the cash-flow problems of a seasonal business. BEA pioneered promotions on midweek travel, off-season fares, 'fly drives' and charter flights in anticipation of the package-holiday boom. 'Holidays for all' ran its campaign at the start of the 1960s.

BEA's efforts to attract new types of customer would have profound consequences for the ways in which it presented itself to the public and how that public, in turn, perceived it. The company's manner had been heavily shaped by the war. When the first British European Airways services took off from RAF Northolt in 1946, the airfield's no-smoking signs were still in Polish, a legacy of the Polish contribution to the Battle of Britain, and passengers carried fur coats to keep themselves warm in the unpressurised planes. By 1960 the experience of Northolt must have appeared a peculiar dream as BEA passengers were shepherded on to a jet via a covered pier at Gatwick, to be welcomed by stewardesses who had ditched their ex-Army jackets

133 BEA
Designer: Adelman
BEA poster, c.1953

134 BEA - British
European Airways
Designer: Ian Ribbons
BEA poster, c.1953

BRITISH EUROPEAN AIRWAYS

**135 For Comfort
Fly BEA**
Unknown designer
BEA poster, c.1946

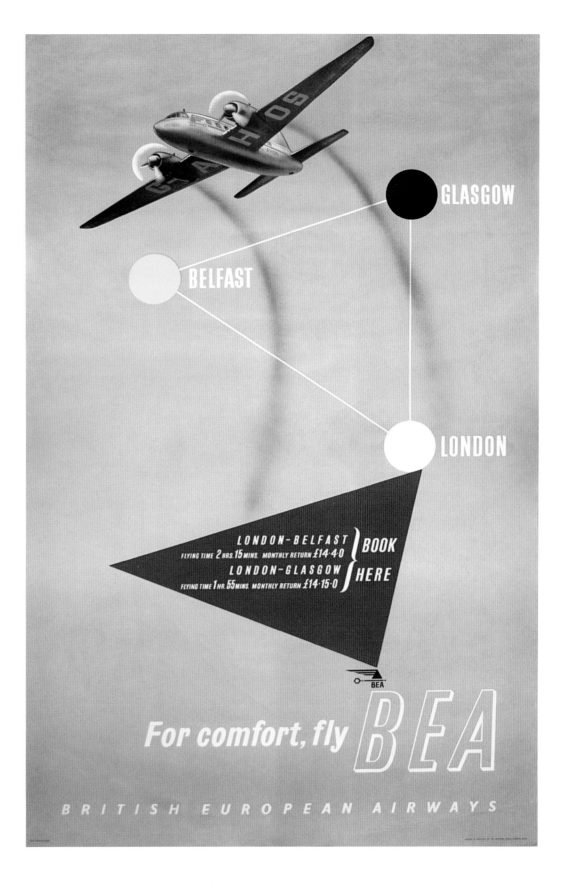

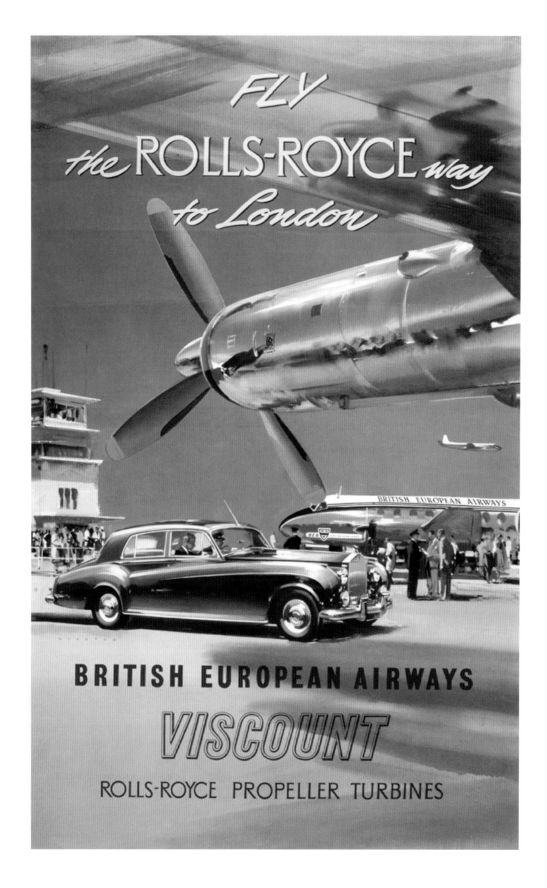

for uniforms inspired by Dior. Britain stood on the cusp of a consumer boom, a boom that undermined the assumptions that the company had been built on. Where once they had been tightly bound into the national fabric because of a national emergency, state companies now had to prove their relevance to a newly affluent Europe.

Early BEA posters evidenced little development on the iconographic tropes established in the inter-war period, with national and international occasions (along with the launch of new British planes) remaining the focus of attention. There were good reasons for this. The introduction of the Vickers Viscount in 1948, with its hybrid part jet, part propeller-driven engine, was the cornerstone of BEA's early success. Aside from its name (it was intended to be called the Viceroy until the partition of India in 1947), everything about the turboprop and its production functioned smoothly, and it was sold around the world, setting new standards in speed and efficiency. *Britain Can Make It* had been the title of the design exhibition at the Victoria and Albert Museum in 1946, and it seemed that it really could. BEA had been fortunate with the government-decreed Viscount in a way that BOAC had not with the Comet. Indeed, even BEA's more off-piste investments, such as helicopters, ultimately proved valuable. While a series of experimental city-to-city helicopter services were a drain on finances, BEA did develop a number of profitable charter services after the opening of the Penzance to Scilly Isles helicopter link in 1964. And later, when the North Sea oil industry began to develop, BEA was able to take full commercial advantage of its slowly acquired expertise. BEA's publicity tapped into a widely shared national pride in technological advancement. The employment of Festival of Britain artists, such as Hugh Casson (1910–99), was evidence of the continuity of its ambitions.

Over the longer term, however, the aesthetic quality of BEA's posters began to decline as it concentrated its advertising on the media forms that most appealed to its changing target audience. By 1951, BEA had become the seventh biggest airline in the world, but despite boasting an impressive list of achievements, for much of the post-war period BEA was looked down upon as the poor relation of British civil aviation. Even though the Viscount operated in the era of all first-class cabins, BEA was not able to make it pay. The demand for short-haul flights proved highly seasonal – three profitable summer months bolstered by tourist traffic were wiped out by winter downturns. As visitor numbers grew and tourist-class fares were introduced in the early 1950s these seasonal peaks and troughs expanded further. Passenger demand in the summer stubbornly remained 12 times as high as demand in the winter. The airline's loss-making, its 'feeder' status and the relative simplicity of flying its routes stood in contrast to BOAC. In comparison with the grandiose task of linking London with North America, Asia, Africa and Australasia, the financial and logistical peculiarities of the short-haul market were not easily appreciated. BEA was never able to hide behind prestige.

Lord Sholto Douglas (1893–1969), Chairman of BEA from 1949 to 1964, would continually and unsympathetically be pressurised by government to place the airline's finances on a sound footing, while also increasing passenger numbers and investing heavily in the nation's aeroplanes and aviation infrastructure. For his part, Douglas felt that BOAC was cosseted by a relative lack of competition and considerable airmail subsidy. 'In congratulating our friends at BOAC for moving into profit ahead of us,' as he put it in 1952, 'we must remember too that our routes are those over which the largest amount of traffic will move in the future. Ours will be the

137 Long-serving Chairman
Lord Sholto Douglas
(right) played a cruicial role
in protecting BEA from
government interference and
the threat of amalgamation with
BOAC. Seen here with Captain
Baillie, *c.*1952.

primary task of providing mass air travel at tourist rates with both fixed wing aircraft and the large helicopters of the future.'[105] This was recognition for BOAC's achievement through gritted (and less favourably remunerated) teeth.

This culmination of factors encouraged a cheap-and-cheerful element to enter BEA's publicity – as if any kind of aesthetic extravagance somehow equated with unwarranted expense and organisational inefficiency. BEA and BOAC had been set up as national flagships – their early promotional items worked as a kind of corporate heraldry. The birth of an international tourist market saw both companies coming to rely much more heavily on photography and employing literal and expositional visual idioms.

As more fuel-efficient planes opened up previously remote areas to mass tourism, profits grew rapidly. 'North Africa, Greece, Malta,

Cyprus, Morocco,' as an air expert had it in 1958, 'are like Nice ten years ago.'[106] By taking a large stake in Cyprus Airways and launching a partnership with Olympic Airways, BEA made a concerted effort to gain a competitive advantage in a fast-growing area. Tourism was understood as a key industry of the future and concerted investment by Near and Middle Eastern governments in places such as Greece, Turkey, Lebanon, Iraq, Saudi Arabia and Syria added a keener edge of competition and further brought down BEA's costs. 'Our booking office is filled all day with travellers from every part of the Levant,' as a BEA clerk in Cyprus had it. 'Veiled woman are among them, rabbis with patriarchal beards, and the busy Beirut merchant with a suitcase full of samples.'[107] In 1958–9 British European Airways had posted a profit of just under £100,000; by 1959–60 its profits had passed £2 million.

138 Fly to Rome by BOAC
Designer: Hugh Casson
BOAC poster, 1955

British European Airways was perhaps the first key patron of Hugh Casson's architectural practice. An early enthusiast for prefabrication, Casson made his name with the Festival of Britain and as an advocate of new building materials. However, he was also an avid sketcher of historic monuments. Casson's iconoclasm was balanced with a restrained elegance that saw him entrusted with a variety of projects for the monarchy, beginning with the street decorations for the coronation of Elizabeth II.

Mary de Saulles and BEA's Red Square

There is a case to be made that in the first decade after the Second World War the most important architectural practice in the world was based at London County Council (LCC). If not the largest architectural organisation in the world, the LCC Architects Department was certainly one of the largest – employing some 3,000 staff (750 of whom were architects). With private business still recovering from the war, there were practical reasons why architects wanted to work in the public sector (as late as 1954, 74 per cent of all dwellings were built by the state), especially as local authorities had been given new responsibilities for house- and school-building programmes.[108] But the LCC Architects Department was also charged with an enormous task that would have stretched ten times as many staff – the reconstruction of a bomb-scarred capital city. It was this heady mixture of idealism and once-in-an-epoch opportunity that briefly made the LCC into one of 'the' places to work, eventually drawing in architects (and their ideas) from Czechoslovakia, Poland, Finland, Sweden and the United States.

Although its architects worked across a full spectrum of styles, the building of the Corbusier inspired Alton estate at Roehampton, south-west London (sometimes visible on the present-day approach into Heathrow), gave the LCC a voguish reputation. Working for three years at the LCC Architects Department under Leslie Martin (1908–2000), arguably the controlling architectural imagination behind the Festival of Britain, was seen as the foundation for a stellar career. The LCC promoted itself as the place where the Inigo Jones, Wrens and Vanbrughs of the modern age developed. It operated as a kind of finishing school for thrusting young modernist architects who had trained at the Architectural Association. This context explains how British European Airways came to appoint two young graduates of the LCC, John Lunn and Mary de Saulles, as their first industrial designers. Mary de Saulles, whom Lunn's bosses had initially refused to shortlist on the basis that 'this is not a job for a woman', would subsequently devise the red square that was to become BEA's trademark.

The red square was the key component of a deliberate attempt to create a 'house style' (the word 'brand' was at this point still primarily associated

140 BEA china dish
Made by Queensbury,
Staffordshire
BEA promoted high-quality
British goods such as
Staffordshire pottery.

141 Fly BEA
Designer: Mary de Saulles
Drawing, c.1954

needed to project itself through the look and ambience of its international chain of ticket offices. This was a British airline attempting to ape the lessons of retailers such as Austin Reed, Simpson's and Harvey Nichols.

Colman, Prentis and Varley had developed the first BEA logo – a maroon key, a literal representation of the fact that BEA was 'the key to Europe' – but not only had this first logo dated quickly, the logic behind its use had changed. In the formulation of Lunn and de Saulles, visual experience and presentation were a constituent part of quality of service and organisational efficiency, not separate from it. The company's new logo was thus to be rebuilt around the letters BEA. The effort to emphasise the visual presence of these letters led to the adoption of strong primary colours and simple geometric forms. The red BEA square was born.

The ingeniousness of de Saulles' house style was that the square was a unit of communication that could be easily adapted, amended and added to. It could be used on posters, luggage labels and furniture. There also seems a connection between the thinking informing the BEA motif and the LCC building of the early post-war period – a correlation between BEA's red square and the slab blocks of concrete flats and maisonettes that the LCC laid out in low-density quadrangles. Equally, the frontages of BEA travel offices very much appear to operate as more highly specified versions of the offices and schools constructed by the LCC in the first decade after the war.

Other aspects of the LCC's influence on BEA require less interpretation. 'Life at the LCC was great fun,' remembered one architect, 'we all did as we pleased, there was no discipline of central control. You just ignored the design briefs and got on with designing what you, as an architect, thought was best for people!'[109] It was a similar

with what were seen as dubious American practices). By developing a house style, BEA wanted to associate itself with a set of new or rapidly evolving industries that valued better product design; it took inspiration from new manufacturing approaches to furniture, radios and domestic consumer goods. It was a development that also recognised that BEA was unable and unwilling to bludgeon customers with multiple advertising campaigns, and instead

142 (Before) BEA shop front, Regent Street, Southampton, c.1952

143 (After) BEA shop front, Southampton, c.1954

Mary de Saulles had been part of the LCC architect's office that was responsible for the post-war redevelopment of the South Bank, expertise that enabled her to give a makeover to BEA's shops as well as the company's corporate identity.

**144 Fly BEA & Olympic –
Greece**
Unknown designer
BEA poster in association with
Olympic, c.1960

**145 Fly BEA – Special
Forces Leave Fares**
Photograph: Anne Hayward
BEA leaflet, c.1956

outward-looking arrogance, in the best sense, that prompted de Saulles to simply ignore the examples of rival airlines, the efforts of which (with the exception of Swissair) she considered fussy and uninspired. Even BOAC's 'Speedbird' got short shrift. 'It was pretty enough', de Saulles remembered, 'but it was just a logo, a clever gimmick.'[110] The BEA emblem was to embody the modernist virtues of design as a practical and problem-solving practice.

Perhaps most astonishingly, Lunn and de Saulles slowly rolled out the red square in piecemeal fashion without the authority of the airline's chiefs. This was significant change through a whispering

146 BEA Helicopter Spraying Service – For the Control of Plight in Potatoes
Designer: Mary de Saulles
Leaflet, c.1958

147 Swinging London: The Beatles disembark from a BEA plane, 1964.

campaign. When an advertising manager, who wanted to replace the red square, was recruited from the boy's magazine the *Eagle*, Lunn and de Saulles pointed him towards market research that found that the red square, BEA's unofficial logo, was the most recognised brand in Britain after Shell. The research paved the way for the logo to be systematically and 'officially' rolled out across Britain and Europe to great acclaim. When Ringo Starr emerged from a BEA plane cheekily holding up a square emblazoned with 'TLES' next to the BEA logo, the airline secured its place in British popular culture.

Acclaim and Crisis: BEA and the Euro Boom

Celebrity would transform the image of aviation during the post-war boom, as surely as the coronation had elevated its status in the years of austerity. Pictures of film stars, celebrities and sportsmen, such as Rock Hudson, Eva Bartok and Joan Greenwood, emerging from airplanes became a staple feature of popular newspapers. The ubiquity of such photographs prompted Mary de Saulles to suggest that a BEA logo should always be placed alongside aeroplane exits to ensure that the company got as much free publicity as possible. This became policy. From whatever angle a BEA plane was seen, its logo was visible. The new liveries developed for Comet 4 and the Vickers Vanguard took such publicity-hungry consideration to a further extreme. There were practical and safety reasons for their distinct new liveries, but its blocks of colour were also consciously designed to look good on television. The company's public relations chief began to talk about BEA as if it too was parked up on Sunset Boulevard. 'An airline is like a film star,' as he put it, 'we must take the rough with smooth; when the press and public begin to ignore us altogether is the time to worry.'[111] Norma

Desmond would have understood. Of course, BEA's brush with stardust could work both ways. Very real tragedy occurred in 1958 when British European Airways Flight 609 crashed on its third attempt to take off from Munich airport. Twenty of the forty-four passengers were killed including eight members of Manchester United's 'Busby Babes'.

By the late 1950s the movies were filling wider screens with ever more sumptuous visual effects as they sought to fend off competition from television. Poster design similarly became brighter, bolder and more aggressively attention-seeking. In BEA's case the opening up of the south Mediterranean encouraged BEA poster designers to adopt palettes that radiated red, orange and yellow. These were posters designed to attract the sun-deprived British public to the eternally blue-skied further regions of Europe. In 1961, BEA's tie-in with the Portuguese airline TAP (Transportes Aéreos Portugueses) came primarily on the back of the Portuguese government's decision to develop the Algarve region as a tourist resort, but the BEA management was also alive to how the changing priorities of the European economy were underpinned by the

148 Fly to Europe This Summer – BEA
Unknown designer
BEA poster, c.1950

fly to Europe this summer

BEA

BRITISH EUROPEAN AIRWAYS   THE KEY TO EUROPE

fly **BEA** to the Sun

FRENCH
RIVIERA

SPAIN

NORTH
AFRICA

ITALY

MAJORCA

MALTA G.C

GREECE

GIBRALTAR

TURKEY

PORTUGAL

CYPRUS

CORSICA

BRITISH EUROPEAN AIRWAYS

149 Fly BEA to the Sun
Designer: M.H. Armengol
BEA poster, c.1950

fly **BEA** to the sun

GIBRALTAR
TANGIER
TRIPOLI
MALTA G.C.

FRENCH RIVIERA
SPAIN
EGYPT
ITALY
MAJORCA
GREECE
TURKEY
PORTUGAL
CORSICA

BRITISH EUROPEAN AIRWAYS

150 Fly BEA to the Sun
Designer: Robert Scanlon
BEA poster, c.1958

growth of civil aviation. 'The first and outstanding fact is that almost the whole of Europe is enjoying what the economists call "growth economy",' aviation experts reasoned, 'while this "growth economy" exists throughout Europe more and more people every year have the money to spend on television sets, refrigerators, motor cars, holidays and, ultimately, air travel.'[112]

Aviation was starting to exert an appreciable influence on Britain's tastes. As the 1960s progressed the expansion of BEA's services fed the new demands of a consumer society. Its flights brought Italian salami to Soho, French button mushrooms to Kensington and medical supplies to National Health Service hospitals. The expansion of its routes further serviced a growing number of trade shows, expos and summits. Perhaps these trends helped explain why the posters of the period looked evermore like shop catalogues. Imperial Airways posters had operated at the aesthetic and intellectual limits of its era; BEA's jostled for attention in a new kind of market. BEA posters can provide interesting snapshots of the day, but although carefully conceived they are rarely executed with the same attention to detail as the finest work produced by its predecessor. The risky aesthetic virtuosity of the pre-war age was in steady decline.

By the dawn of the 1960s BEA occupied a strange position in the public mind. It had become a conduit of a kind of cosmopolitan consumerism, but it was also the subsidised national flag-carrier and was on occasions lambasted in the press for its lack of patriotism. In the firm's early years it had directly assisted the government during times of national crisis – for example, its planes had taken part in the 1948 Berlin airlift – but by the late 1950s BEA's relationship with the British state was less clear. Indeed, the expansion of tourist routes to the Near and Middle East coupled with the process of decolonisation led BEA to err on the side of caution when it came to asserting its 'Britishness', even removing the Union Jack (to the distaste of newspaper critics) from its promotional literature. BEA believed it was acting rationally. Market research had suggested that in the short-haul market there was little economic gain in investing heavily in a distinctive passenger experience, 'British' or otherwise. American dominance on Atlantic routes offered BOAC a 'British' niche to exploit, but the idea of Europe did not hold the same imaginative weight with the British public and BEA struggled to create a visual identity that so easily flattered national pride. The political price of becoming an internationally significant airline, then, was a more problematic relationship with the United Kingdom.

While BEA was criticised for its lack of patriotism, it also found itself accused of failing British consumers. The formation of British United Airlines in 1960 exemplified a new direction in government thinking. Now shipping and aviation interests were being encouraged by the state to compete with BEA and BOAC. Lord Douglas was furious. BEA had been established as a national carrier when there was a consensus that a national business should view economic activity in the round, negotiating the needs of research, manufacturer, distributor and customer into a mutually beneficial compromise. In Douglas' view, more private entrants would both undermine a national success story and siphon public investment into private pockets. He understood that the emergence of rivals such as British Caledonian and British United was a consequence of massive trial-and-error investment in the national aviation infrastructure, and was frustrated that the rapid rise of the independents was now taken as proof of the failure (rather than the success) of the subsidised national flag-carriers. With their siren call of lower prices and greater competition, new commercial airlines were to become dangerous rivals to BEA as the decade progressed. BEA's simple and sales-orientated publicity had enabled it to achieve impressive results but it had also undermined an understanding of the exceptional nature of its achievements. This dilemma reflected a broader political change.

It had taken BEA nine years to carry its first ten million passengers but less than four to carry its second. After years of being castigated as a failure, BEA had become a profitable airline. But what might have been a story of achievement was coming to be seen more ambiguously. According to a new generation of politicians, national cartels needed to be animated by competition (rather than cooperation). Recession in the United States would kick the difficulty of disentangling 'national interest' and 'consumer interest' into the political mid-distance. Until the nationalised airlines were finally relieved of their duty to buy British aeroplanes, and while the International Air Transport Association (IATA) retained the ability to set global ticket prices, the old consensus held, although the question of how a national industry should properly serve the nation, and whether this relationship needed to be redefined, would not go away. In time, the post-war definition would fall out of favour as the rapid realisation of profit would be adjudged as being of greatest benefit to the nation. This was a massive attitudinal shift. The self-image projected by BEA's design from the late 1950s, and the way in which BEA communicated with the public through its posters, its airplanes and its buildings, provide an interesting material record of how this shift in attitude, a shift that was to have ever more significant consequences as the century progressed, began to make itself felt.

151 Passengers' luggage is loaded onto a bus at BEA's west London air terminal, opened in 1957

152 BOAC Guide to Inclusive Tours All Over the World – Ask Here for Your Free Copy
Unknown designer
BOAC poster, c.1956

The Sixties Begin to Swing

It is 1963. Fog descends over London Airport. Flights are grounded and the great and the good waiting to fly to New York make their way into the VIP lounge. A famous actress was set to leave her husband and fly off with her young lover, but the bad weather had given him a final chance to win back her love. 'For thirteen years I have mostly loved him,' frets the actress, 'but I don't know him.'

This was the plot of *The VIPs*, an Oscar-winning blockbuster starring Richard Burton, Elizabeth Taylor and Orson Welles. The film was shot at London Airport's new Oceanic Terminal (now Heathrow's Terminal 3) and marked the birth of a glamorous new phase in the airport's existence. (The voyeuristic kick to Terence Rattigan's melodrama was that it was reputedly based on Vivien Leigh's attempt to leave Laurence Olivier.) With its marble floors and upscale cocktail bars, the Oceanic Terminal had become a place to be seen. Less than 20 years earlier, the airport had been just rows of tents. The remarkable reinvention of Heathrow tells something of the story of how British aviation, perceptions of aviation and the self-image of aviation had altered.

London Airport had opened on 1 January 1946 when a BSAA plane took off for Buenos Aires, reopening 18 days later when the plane returned. The laying of the airport's thick concrete runway, rightly judged a prerequisite for the post-war world to come, had begun two years earlier. Originally planned as a new long-haul RAF base to serve the conflict in the Far East, the airport was adapted for civilian use by George Wimpey & Co., the Home Guard and a small number of German prisoners-of-war. At the staggering cost of £25 million (around £870 million at today's prices) it would represent the new Labour administration's largest building project. Travellers may have had to suffer the tents, but its sophisticated 'Star of David' runway pattern meant that planes, unaffected by wind, could take off in any direction at any time. The town planner Patrick Abercrombie (1879–1957), founding father of London's green belt, set aside further room for an Underground link, an express train service and a third runway which would likely be required in the future. Despite its shabby passenger facilities this was the world's largest and costliest airport.

153 Jet BOAC to Swinging London
Unknown designer
BOAC poster, c.1966

154 Laying the runway at Heathrow: Wimpey, the Home Guard and German POWs, c.1946.

It is worth contrasting the atmosphere of London Airport with 'London Heathrow', the airport it would become in 1966. A journalist wrote in 1948:

> Buildings push up like mothballs and disappear just as quickly. Old houses, too, on the outskirts of the field are suffering the fate of vanished Heath Row, and their shells, with old strips of wallpaper hanging from them, are perhaps the nearest thing to a symbol which London Airport has to show. Their steady destruction gives the feeling that here were those undisciplined and unorganised boxes of soft people, chock full of 'human error' used to live; while the future only belongs to the great impersonal hangars, where perfect machines can live in perfect functional surroundings.[113]

The knowingly romantic tone seems a little forced, but the article does convey the rapidity with which

Heathrow developed from a hamlet of houses to a configuration of runways surrounded by tents, then caravans and prefabs, and then permanent buildings. London Airport's form began to solidify in 1955 with the opening of the Europa Building (which became Terminal 2) by Frederick Gibberd (1908–84). Now best known for Didcot's remarkable power station and his work on Harlow New Town, Gibberd was then one of Britain's most celebrated modernist architects. His building, the first 'permanent' building at the airport (it was demolished in 2011) inaugurated a new phase in the airport's history. The Europa Building, with its long viewing platform, a roof garden, and a commentator describing the airfield movements, became a popular family day out. At one point Gibberd's pioneering building attracted more visitors than Madame Tussauds and the Tower of London. In 1956 more than one million people paid to spend an afternoon at London Airport.

The glamour phase celebrated by *The VIPs* coincided with a governmental drive to turn London Airport into a profitable business. This would culminate in the creation of the British Airports Authority and London Airport becoming 'Heathrow'. The growth of passenger numbers and a new money-making impetus brought rapid improvements to passenger facilities. This strategy may have resulted in what visionary architect Reyner Banham described as Heathrow's 'landscape of hysteria', and it might have delayed the extension of the Underground network (Heathrow Central opened for the Queen's Jubilee in 1977) and a fast rail link (Heathrow Express began operation in 1998), but it transformed the airport. In 1964 the Beatles' arrival at London Airport was broadcast live on television as 4,000 screaming fans greeted the Fab Four on their return from the United States. This was a watershed moment. London Airport,

155 'Tent city' – the early years at London Heathrow, 1946

The transformation of Heathrow into one of the world's major airports began with Lord Balfour's decision to requisition Hounslow farmland in 1944, ostensibly to build a base for

long-range aircraft to service the war against Japan. Eleven years later 'tent city' had made way for Frederick Gibberd's Europa Terminal – and the airport's pub (The Bricklayer's Arms) was renamed The Air Hostess.

156 Frederick Gibberd's control tower and terminal at Heathrow airport, c.1955

along with Carnaby Street and the Cavern nightclub, had become a British 'destination'. Twelve ornate chandeliers were given pride of place in the lobby of the new Oceanic Building.

As far as civil aviation is concerned, the 1960s were about more than glamour; serenity was also given a new definition. This was the tale told by BOAC's advertising for its new signature aeroplane: the Vickers VC-10. The VC-10 was developed as Britain's distinctive answer to the Boeing 707. With its rear-mounted engines the plane was purposely designed to be different. There were palpable advantages to placing the engines at the back of the plane – clear wings made for a smoother, quieter flight and the plane could take off from shorter runways (still an issue in parts of the Commonwealth) at lower speeds. The 'velvet-voiced' VC-10 offered passengers a quiet and comfortable flight amongst interiors designed by Gaby Schreiber (c.1916 –91), in a cabin where temperature was controlled, like a giant refrigerator, by two giant vapour pumps. Schreiber's interior was regarded at the time as a masterstroke. Cabins had tended to be themed according to the presumed mindset of 'business' or 'holiday' travellers but Schreiber modelled her interior on a hotel, theorising that passengers deprived of their independence during the journey needed a mixture of relaxation and stimulation. Her job was to build an environment that would prevent boredom and claustrophobia, enabling stewardesses to meet any conceivable passenger need. If the revolutionary speed of jet-propulsion had been Comet's calling card, BOAC promoted its iconic intercontinental service of the 1960s as offering customers 'VC ten-derness'.

The smooth introduction of the VC-10 in 1964 nevertheless hid a period of considerable internal turmoil. The withdrawal of the Comet had seen

BOAC slip from being the most technologically advanced airline in the world to one whose fleet was distinctly second class. Worse, BOAC's ageing, second-hand fleet had been bought at considerable expense, as international competitors cashed in on BOAC's misfortune. The VC-10 and its successor, the Super VC-10, had been ordered in 1957 against the wishes of Basil Smallpeice and the BOAC board.[114] The VC-10 was imposed on BOAC by a government that wanted it to buy British rather than Boeing, but, after the trauma of Comet, BOAC management wanted to steer company priorities away from being the first to being the best. The key tension was between BOAC who wanted British manufacturers to produce the Boeing under licence and British manufacturers who wanted to produce something that made full use of their much-admired ingenuity. The distinctiveness of the VC-10 proved an iconic strength for BOAC, but despite entering service several years later, in terms of seating, weight and fuel economy it was still not

a match for the 707. The VC-10 would be much loved by pilots and passengers, but ultimately it was not beneficial to the BOAC balance sheet.[115]

The VC-10 was to prove a symbolic case. The Macmillan government (1957–63) had given new financial and economic obligations to the nationalised industries. Dividends had to be paid to government even when losses were made and in the run up to elections government was minded to cut the budgets of nationalised industries to

157 Triumphantly Swift, Silent, Serene – the BOAC VC-10
Unknown designer, artwork by Frank Wootton.
BOAC poster, c.1966

158 Interior of the Comet 4
Photograph, c.1958

159 The Concorde - the world's first supersonic passenger jet - on show in Hong Kong, *c.*1966.

160 BOAC flight deck simulator, *c.*1966

increase the budgetary surplus. BOAC was being simultaneously ordered to maximise short-term profits and provide British manufacturers with long-term support. Something of the political schizophrenia of the period was demonstrated by official attitudes towards the first research into supersonic air travel that was conducted in the early 1960s. Government subsidised the development of what would become the fabulous-but-frighteningly-expensive Concorde, but despite recognising that Concorde would prove a financial burden, it dispensed with the services of Basil Smallpiece on the grounds that BOAC was not profitable enough.

Supersonic travel was not the only transformative technology to emerge in 1960s. Scientists at the Blind Landing Experimental Unit at Bedford developed the technologies necessary for all-weather flying. The Gust Research Unit began to probe the small pockets of turbulence that existed at high altitudes. The formation of a United Nations forum for the peaceful uses of outer space peered ahead to the days when weather observational satellites would provide pilots with meteorological updates in real-time. What was true of BOAC and BEA's air operations was true for their administrators as the 1960s saw what *BOAC Magazine* described as the advance of 'electronic brains'. Manual booking and records were gradually being replaced by press-button technology, as fares, mileage, route maps, notes and regulations began to be fed into the company's new IBM650 computers. Business processes began to speed up as computers were used to provide weekly and monthly updates of estimates of revenue.

As the wartime generation began to retire it was replaced by a generation that employed work studies and planned staff rationalisations in response to the continuing political pressure to reduce costs. Along with companies such as Cadbury's,

Unilever, Ford and EMI, BOAC began to allot market research a central role in determining management strategy. This 'scientific' approach to management saw the company begin to think of itself, and its services, less as a whole and more in terms of a number of constituent parts that could be individually controlled. Although BOAC made a series of heavy losses in the early 1960s (losing £12.2 million in 1963, despite a 9.3 per cent rise in passenger numbers), its management was reassured by the constant gains in capacity and efficiency. The effective sacking of the old BOAC board temporarily abated political pressure. It was now

a question of waiting for the economic cycle to turn.

Changes in civil aviation during the 1960s illustrate a neat paradox. The Swinging Sixties is usually shorthand for the explosion of pop culture, and the boom in consumer goods and international fashions – trends which the growth in aviation arguably underpinned – yet these developments rested on organisational norms moving relentlessly in an altogether less flamboyant, more rationalised and instrumental direction. One vision of aviation in the 1960s might focus on the 'Motown jet', the BOAC plane that bought a revue of touring Motown artists such as Marvin Gaye, Smokey Robinson and the Supremes to the UK for the first time.[116] Another version of aviation in the 1960s would focus on the introduction of high-speed cargo-loading and mechanised baggage-handling.

Greater mechanisation meant that retiring war-era workers in labour-intensive jobs tended to be replaced by new sales staff, with free holidays offered as rewards to those who performed exceptionally well. The establishment and then expansion of BOAC's Sales Training Centre in Old Burlington Street, London, was part of a renewed emphasis on growth. One effect of this was to make marketing material much more self-consciously utilitarian; it had obviously and immediately to 'sell itself' to the public. 'We live in a buyer's market, not a seller's market,' declared *BOAC Magazine*.[117]

During the 1960s tourism would become Britain's fifth biggest industry. Visitors from North America were crucial to this growth. The enormous popularity of group travel and package European tours in the United States meant that BOAC began to reshape its offering towards American tastes. Going into the 1960s, North American passengers accounted for a third of BOAC's overall total, while two-thirds of sales on Western routes were paid for in dollars. During the 1960s not only was the number of people sailing across the Atlantic finally surpassed by the number flying over it, but the Boeing 707 came to be the signature airplane of the transatlantic journey. BOAC had ordered Boeing 707s primarily because they were exceptional airplanes that brought clear economic and technological advantages, but there was another rationale at work. Large numbers of North Americans flew with BOAC and if they preferred to fly in a Boeing 707 then their preferences could not be easily dismissed. In the 1950s the 'Britishness' of BOAC and BEA's fleets had often been the focus of their adverts; in the future that Britishness was to be confined to some of their components – for instance, the use of Rolls-Royce engines. The holistic approach to British civil aviation of the early post-war period was slowly being chipped away.

**163 South America,
fly there by BOAC**
Unknown designer
BOAC poster, 1959

A colourful promotion of
BOAC's South American
service, restored in 1958
after a four year gap caused
by a shortage of aircraft
following the Comet disasters.
The poster highlights carnival
time in Rio de Janeiro with
its costumes, masks and
decorations, all exciting and
exotic prospects for Britons
who, according to Prime
Minister Harold Macmillan,
had 'never had it so good'.
The British were better off but
jet-set holidays in Brazil were
still for the affluent few.

**164 Scotland,
Fly BOAC**
Unknown designer
BOAC poster, c.1959

Most BOAC posters aimed
at the North American
market highlighted the tourist
attractions of London or
the English countryside,
but this shows a belated
recognition of the appeal of
Scotland, particularly to those
in the USA and Canada with
family connections through
generations of emigrants.
It is also an unusually strong
graphic design from a period
when posters were in rapid
decline as a medium and
increasingly reliant on bland
photographic images.

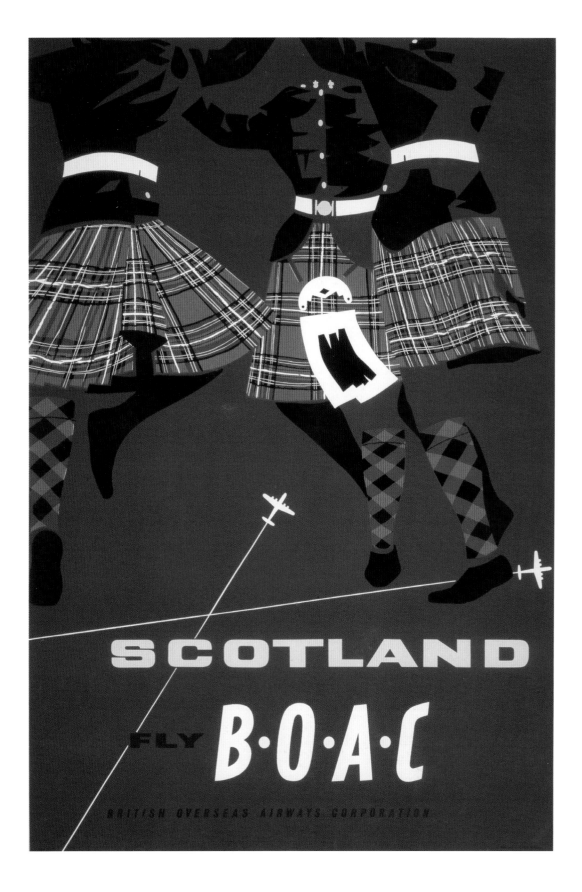

SCOTLAND

FLY B·O·A·C

BRITISH OVERSEAS AIRWAYS CORPORATION

The New Frontiers of Design

Looking through BOAC and BEA posters from the 1960s it's striking how far the airline's norms were changing. BOAC began to sell itself and Britain in terms thought to have the greatest appeal to Americans. With millions of dollars at stake BOAC had begun to study the preferences of North American customers. Its investigations included what brought North Americans to Britain, what might bring more of them and how these interests could be commercially exploited. BOAC posters such as 'Britain: The Gateway to Europe' and 'Europe is for Fun' are testaments to this. One interesting sideline of this trend was research BOAC did on the appeal of genealogy to North Americans, but the operation of BOAC's Cabin School, which became the focus of a popular BBC documentary of the time, is more typical. Research had revealed that for North Americans, 'British men are gallant and dashing – easy to get on with, more mature and much more attractive than other men.' The typical British woman, by contrast, 'chooses styles which are too old for her years. In America women wear much more youthful fashions and dowdiness is rare.'[118] Such insights led to BOAC exploiting the image of pilots and rethinking the uniforms of its stewardesses.

It is difficult to imagine a definition of dowdy that would include the fireproof paper mini-shift dresses introduced on BOAC's VC-10 service between New York and the Caribbean in 1967. The green, jewelled slippers, flower in the hair and white gloves of the short skirt-wearing stewardesses departing from JFK exist in a parallel universe to the navy blue suit and white blouse of the standard BOAC uniform of the time. 'The girls can decide for themselves how high they want the hemline,' *BOAC News* informed staff, 'within limits, of course.'[119] (The limit was later revealed to be not more than three inches above the knee.) BOAC was making a conscious attempt to tap into the symbols of New Britishness.

The style of air stewardesses had changed dramatically in the 20 years following the Second World War. BOAC had stepped tentatively towards American norms when it began employing women as stewardesses in 1946. Reflecting the military background of this first cohort, stewardesses were required to change out of their blue uniform

165 Hardy Amies' sensational 'red hood' uniform for BEA, c.1967

166 BOAC stewardesses learn make-up skills at Cranebank training centre, *c.*1966.

travellers required a rethinking of the steward's role. Affordability was now less of a barrier to air travel than willingness to fly. Stewardesses had an important part to play in creating a positive atmosphere, bringing a human touch to an increasingly complex technical and industrial enterprise. The stewardess played a crucial role in what might be termed the psychology of celebrity identification. 'The idea is that if you photograph a film star doing anything, you automatically win the public's confidence in the things she's doing,' a BEA marketing man had noted, 'washing her face with Somebody's Soap or dousing her food in Somebody else's Sauce.'[120] As aviation developed an important part of the stewardesses' role came to be performative – her job was to instil confidence and radiate happiness about the experience of flying.

The attire of the British stewardess altered as swiftly as her status. From 1960 designing a new uniform became an important fashion moment. BEA and BOAC employed the likes of Sylvia Ayton, Clive Evans and Norman Hartnell; in recent times Roland Klein, Paul Costelloe and Julien Macdonald have designed outfits for British Airways. One especially notable uniform of the 1960s was the 'Red Riding Hood Look' designed by Hardy Amies, dressmaker to Queen Elizabeth II. This was a striking scarlet zip-up hooded top, designed to match the red wings of BEA's new livery, worn over a royal blue dress. It gave perhaps the smallest inkling of the concept of 'power dressing' that Amies was later to perfect.

There's a clear correlation between the decline in the aesthetic qualities of BOAC's posters and the rise of new management techniques (as well as new media forms). But in addition to witnessing the birth of the high-fashion stewardess, the 1960s were arguably also the zenith of distinctive cabin design. Interior furnishings were one obvious area

167 BOAC stand at 'British Week' exhibition, Tokyo, 1969

and into white mess gear whilst preparing and serving meals. The rather forbidding recruitment drive had run under the line 'No glamour girls required'. To further protect the dignity of these workers BEA for a time insisted on dropping the 'ess' from stewardess, even persuading the popular magazine *Picture Post* to run a feature emphasising a BEA steward's linguistic, navigational and medical training. But the growth in numbers of where native expertise could find a distinctive outlet as BOAC and BEA looked for niche areas where they could develop a competitive advantage over rival American carriers. Thus, while the 1960s saw the waning of Abram Games' star, industrial designers such as Robin Day (1915–2010) rose to prominence.

Robin Day had first found acclaim in 1948 when Mies van der Rohe awarded him an international prize for furniture design at the Museum of Modern Art in New York, but it was with his plywood chairs for the 1951 Festival of Britain that he first found wider fame.[121] Making use of modern materials – especially innovations in plastic – Day's work found favour for being recognisably modern without being off-puttingly outré. Heavily influenced by Scandinavian design, his stacking chairs retained enough credibility to be sold in Liberty, but remained practical enough to become a fixture of post-war schools, canteens and conference halls. Day began working with Vickers on the interior of the Super VC-10 at the earliest stage, which gave him previously undreamt of input into the ergonomics of airplane furniture. BOAC wanted the Super VC-10 to eschew what it described as the 'gilts galore' approach of its rivals; it aspired towards something classy, comfortable and 'British'. Day had worked on seating for the Royal Festival Hall in London, the Royal Shakespeare Company theatre in Stratford-upon-Avon and the Mexico City Olympic stadium. This was the sort of company that BOAC wanted to keep.

The advent of the consumer society had altered the configuration of homes and the social patterns of the nation. Responding to these changes, Day had expanded his range of furniture for the home into TV sets and TV loungers, which replaced armrests with small oblong trays for snacking. This work proved an excellent apprenticeship for one of his most important BOAC commissions, the design of a refreshment tray for use on the 707, complete with cutlery, crockery and drinking glasses. Day recalled:

This was an interesting exercise in logistics, as economy of space and weight are crucial to the economics of operating passenger aircraft. Relationships of dimensions and stacking were essential on several levels: firstly, the compact fitting of vessels and implements on trays; secondly, the exact accommodation of trays on mobile trolleys; and thirdly, the accommodation of this equipment, on the galley, on the airfield and in the airport.[122]

Television and tourism really had become the garlands of the New Elizabethan age.

Robin Day was also appointed by BOAC because of the values with which he was personally associated. An iconic vodka advert of the time has Robin and his equally significant designer wife Lucienne posing archly together. 'When not more actively engaged in designing highly idiosyncratic furniture and textiles,' the copy reads, 'Robin and Lucienne Day are apt to be entertaining visitors from Europe or America ... Smirnoff Vodka is invariably accepted with alacrity.' The Days were celebrated in the media for their collaborative work on the interior of John Lewis stores and the refurbishment of new BOAC planes. Indeed, the public and professional image cultivated by Robin and Lucienne made them into a celebrated couple. The Days' back-to-back easels, in the Chelsea studio they shared for many decades, spoke of a whole new model of working relationships. Together they exemplified a personable, sophisticated mid-century brochure Britain which BOAC could uncontroversially sell.

168 Caribbean, USA,
Canada & Mexico
– Jet There by BOAC
Unknown designer
BOAC poster, 1967

Be chary of other airline chairs.

The seat you're expected to sit on for several hours without a stretch is rarely brought to your notice. The reason's simple: most airline chairs are virtually identical, so there's nothing to say about them. Except for ours. BOAC are in the fortunate position of offering the best economy seat in the world. On a long trip, you'll be glad you knew about it. We took the international rules on airline seat design and interpreted them with imagination. For our troubles, we got the first economy seat that doesn't feel 2nd class. Now it's standard on all our planes. Most of our passengers have noticed it. And feel chary about anything else as a result. We think you will. See your BOAC travel agent.

Specially shaped headrest.

Carefully contoured back.

Light weight frame cuts down the bulk making more room for you.

More ship room.

Legroom enough for a six-foot-sixer.

➤ BOAC
takes good care of you

169 Be Chary of Other Chairs
Chair designer: Robin Day
BOAC press advert, 1968

'When I showed [the poster] to them, they said it's much too good for us, we don't want it, what we need is a poster which is part of a total campaign in the press and on television,' remembered designer Frédéric Henri Kay Henrion (1914–90). The BOAC consultant was looking back over the changes that began to sweep through the design industry at the start of the 1960s. During the first decades of the post-war period the necessity of good design to successful business had been established.

But while nearly every major company now had a unified presentational style, they now wanted that style to take its lead from the most expensive, and therefore most prestigious, element of its presentational face – its television adverts. If certain actors were used in a television commercial, then those actors should be featured in the posters. 'I realised,' Henrion reflected sadly, 'it was the end of what I called the ideas poster.'[123] Artists like Henrion, who had worked so-hard to establish the importance of a unified approach to corporate communication, became suddenly vulnerable. Their artistic skills and exceptional craftsmanship appeared less applicable to the new media age.

For 40 years Imperial Airways, BSAA, BEA and BOAC had been brilliant and farsighted patrons of poster design, but posters had increasingly been displaced by photography as the company came to prize functional publicity materials that could be re-purposed for use in magazines, newspapers and as point-of-sale material. Instead, as BOAC's fleet was slowly standardised, and increasingly Americanised, the company's high-end 'Britishness' would be asserted in its interiors. Prominent British designers like the Days, James Gardner and Gaby Schrieber were gradually to supplant Bristol, Vickers and de Havilland as the authors of the company's corporate personality. Civil aviation had become an increasingly specialised business that operated to pan-national standards. Aesthetic standards were universally higher but the employ of distinctive artists had become a niche activity. The visionary sweep of British civil aviation's earliest publicity had been displaced and even the names BOAC and BEA soon disappeared, with their amalgamation into British Airways in 1974. The art of flight was no longer the preserve of an avant-garde elite. It had transformed into an all-pervasive style.

the big round world of
BOAC

170 **The Big Round World of BOAC – Israel**
Unknown designer
BOAC poster, c.1966

ISRAEL

Europe · N.America · S.America · Asia · Australasia · Africa

**171 BOAC 747 – More
Sitting Room in the Sky**
Unknown designer
BOAC poster, c.1971

Epilogue

By the turn of the millennium the 'Britishness' of British civil aviation had altered radically. Britishness now apparently resided in the bright geometric patterns that adorned the houses of the Ndebele tribe in Africa, in a Poole Pottery dolphin sketched by Sally Tuffin, in a poem about the vagaries of the wind by the Chinese calligrapher Yip Man-Yam and in a panel created by the Egyptian artist Chant Avedissian that paid homage to the symmetrical patterns of Islam. Britishness also resided in 47 other eclectic and strikingly individual tailfin designs that were unveiled as the new symbols of British Airways in 1997.

Aviation had, of course, always been an international enterprise but post-cold war 'globalisation' had utterly transformed it. As the European Union and the United States pushed for the radical liberalisation of national airspaces, and as 'super alliances' between national carriers grew in ambition and complexity, it became ever more difficult to delineate what British civil aviation might mean. That British Airways, the successor of Imperial Airways, BEA and BOAC, has now come together with the Spanish carrier Iberia into

the International Airlines Group (IAG) indicates the scale of change that has occurred over the past 30 years.

'Project Utopia', the rebranding of the British Airways fleet in to a number of ethnically distinct liveries, such as the one designed by Yip Man-Yam, represented an ambitious attempt to synthesise, aestheticise and celebrate these changes in a manner that added up to something more substantive than the short-lived corporate fad for 'Glocalisation'. The artists' designs for individual aircraft tailfins were overseen by the London-based design agency Newell and Sorrell, who at the same time introduced the 'Speedmarque' logo in place of the short-lived 'Speedwing', which had finally ousted the Speedbird as BA's corporate emblem in 1984. The various tailfin designs were simultaneously unveiled in New York, London, Seattle, Scotland, Germany and Zimbabwe, and globecast by satellite to parties everywhere from Birmingham to Buenos Aires, Poland to Paris, Toronto to Tokyo, and Glasgow to Geneva. A flotilla of barges – with their sails reflecting BA's new liveries – sailed up a river in Thailand, while a huge dhow featuring

the airline's Middle East world image sailed
into Dubai.

'British Airways remains proudly British,' the
then Chief Executive Robert Ayling explained,
'but perhaps we need to lose some of our old
fashioned Britishness and take on board some
of the new British traits. Abroad, people see this
country as friendly, diverse and open to other
cultures. We must better reflect that.'

The art of British civil aviation had apparently
rediscovered the idealism of Auguste Perret, who
on hearing the news that Louis Blériot had crossed
the Channel, triumphantly declared, 'Wars are
finished: no more wars are possible! There are no
longer any frontiers!'[124]

Not everyone was so enthusiastic. The reaction
of the British media (and sections of the public)
was at points aggressively hostile, including,
tellingly, that of Margaret Thatcher, who had
privatised British Airways and thus set in motion
decisive changes in what the 'Britishness' of the
airline meant.

The repainting of one of BA's fleet with the
Chatham Dockyard's union flag livery for use
by Queen Elizabeth II (the design had originally
been reserved for Concorde) marked the gradual
retreat from Project Utopia. By 1999 the ethnic
liveries were being repainted red, white and blue.

BA eventually sold their stake in the London Eye, and by doing so ended their connection with Robert Ayling's bold experiments in cultural patronage. The unhappy saga was a powerful reminder that, while the carriers, planes and organisational norms of British civil aviation may have been increasingly homogenised by a global market, the psychological and emotional need for British civil aviation to retain its own distinct identity remained.

In the Edwardian period aviation had been a cottage industry that harboured a mixture of cranks, showmen and visionaries; aviation was an attempt to take a giant leap in to the sci-fi future from the bottom of the garden shed. The character of British aviation, which critics of Project Utopia felt was being lost, was the product of two world wars, when heavy investment along with the nurturing of domestic expertise led to both technological innovation and new techniques of mass production. Shorn of government finance, civil aviation had often struggled to remain profitable in peacetime, thus official patronage and national service wore heavily on the character of British aviation. Aviation shrank the globe, bringing nations into closer contact, and the Speedbird symbol first developed by Imperial Airways became a visual representation of Britain's changing place in the world. Speedbird joined together Flying Boats and Empire Air Mail with BOAC's Comet and then Concorde.

Post-war ideological shifts bit hard into the notion of there being any such thing as British civil aviation. Defenders of the old consensus described the privatisation of British Airways as 'looting' and 'piracy', but it was a move that doggedly followed a new kind of logic. After deregulation, British aviation was increasingly also represented by publicity-hungry entrepreneurs such as Freddie Laker, Richard Branson and Stelios Haji-Ioannou.

175 Joan Collins appeared in British Airways adverts in the mid-1980s

The rise of this assertive new breed marked a return to the image of aviation past: to when Alan Cobham and Amy Johnson were mobbed by crowds, to when famous planes held pride of place in Selfridges, to when press barons drummed up public interest in individual spectacle. But the idealism of Perret, and indeed the deregulators, proved misplaced – frontiers remained. The tragic events of 9/11, which led to a renewed emphasis on the importance of national security, look to have brought to a close both the exuberance and excesses that characterised aviation at the turn of the century. British Airways commissioning of artists such as Chant Avedissian already appears a very long time ago. The recent global downturn has further encouraged consolidation. British Airways still exists as an independent brand and its most recent TV and cinema advertising has emphasised BA's place in the reassuring history of British civil aviation even as it moves down a new organisational path.

'Flying was more an art than a science,' the American aviator Charles Lindbergh said back in 1942, 'now it is more a science that an art. It has passed from the era of the pioneer to the era of the

routine operator, from the time when a "good pilot" forgot his instruments in an emergency to the time when a "good pilot" turns to his instruments in an emergency.'[125] Fast forward to the present and aviation has become a ubiquitous part of the modern landscape. The celebrated American town planner, Dr John D. Kasarda, has even argued that the Aerotropolis – a city whose form, infrastructures and industries are built around an airport – represents the future organisation of human civilisation. The internet age, according to this vision, has facilitated a growing need to travel as well as trade. The greater number of pan-national electronic communications that people have, the larger the desire for human contact. Aviation thus has a pivotal role in piecing together what Kasarda calls 'the physical internet'.

How would such a future affect the British Art of Flight? The relentless progress of aviation seems likely to further dilute the wonder of flying and increase nostalgia for the world of civil aviation that has been lost. Environmental concerns will also have a crucial determining influence. The development of enormous super-transporters of people such as the Airbus A380 provides a stark contrast to the motivations that inspired the Comet or Concorde, revealing an industry that is increasingly focused, for both ethical and economic reasons, on reducing its ecological cost. Deregulation has also led to the rise in importance of so-called 'hub airports' that both concentrate the environmental pressures aviation exerts and allow the possibility that these pressures can be thoughtfully managed. Flying may become even more commonplace and unremarkable, but as it does so its broader social responsibilities will once again loom larger. The early art of aviation made much of the fact that flying lifted you above the earth but British Airways' commissioning of prominent land artists such as Andy Goldsworthy speaks of a new and widely shared desire to be more at one with it: this is aviation as a fundamental but increasingly discreet part of the twenty-first-century world. Art and science can never be as cleanly split apart as Lindbergh quipped, but the old Art of Flight chronicled in this book has already been replaced by the new Science of Flight and the new arts which that entails.

Notes

Taking to the Air: From Pioneers to Speedbird *Oliver Green*

1. Wilbur Wright (1867–1912) and Orville Wright (1871–1948). The brothers achieved the world's first powered flight in a heavier than air machine on 17 December 1903. They tossed a coin and it was Orville who piloted their *Flyer* on this historic occasion. It took to the air for 12 seconds, travelling 120 feet (37 m). As one of the witnesses reportedly said, 'Damned if they ain't flew!'

2. Sir George Cayley (1773–1857) designed an 'aerial carriage' with four rotating wings at Brompton Hall, near Scarborough, in 1843. Ten years later he constructed a large tri-plane glider on which his coachman was persuaded to ride. The reluctant aviator did leave the ground briefly but broke his leg on landing. He apparently told Sir George, 'I wish to give notice. I was hired to drive not fly!'

3. For example, H.G. Wells' *The War in the Air* (1908) and F.S. Brereton's *The Great Aeroplane* (1911).

4. Alfred Harmsworth, 1st Viscount Northcliffe (1865–1922) was an early pioneer of tabloid journalism. He began publishing the *Daily Mail* in 1896, founded the *Daily Mirror* in 1903 and acquired *The Times* in 1908, making him the most influential press baron of his day.

5. Quoted in Graham Smith, *Taking to the Skies: The Story of British Aviation 1903–1939*, Countryside Books, Newbury, 2003, p.58.

6. Le Corbusier (pseudonym of Charles Jeanneret-Gris, 1887–1965) recalled this episode in his book *Aircraft*, The Studio, London, 1935. In 1909 he had been a young trainee architect in Perret's office. By 1935, as one of the leading advocates of new international 'machine age' architecture, he had become a great supporter of aviation because it offered a new perspective on the built world below: 'The airplane, advance guard of the conquering armies of the New Age, the airplane arouses our energies and our faith.'

7. Thomas Sopwith (1888–1989) won a £4,000 prize for the longest flight from England to the Continent in 1910. He used his winnings to set up the Sopwith School of Flying at Brooklands and in 1912 established the Sopwith Aviation Company, which produced more than 18,000 aircraft during the First World War. He later established Hawker Aircraft.

8. Website of Aldershot Military Museum, http://www.hants.gov.uk/Aldershot-museum/local-history-aldershot [accessed 1 December 2011].

9. Claude Grahame-White (1879–1959) made the first night flight in Britain during the *Daily Mail* sponsored London to Manchester Air Race of 1910. He had learned to fly in France in 1909 and was one of the first Englishmen to qualify as a pilot. The RAF Museum now occupies part of the aerodrome site he established at Hendon and has reconstructed one of his First World War aircraft factory hangars to house part of its collection.

10. Frank Pick (1878–1941) was an outstanding transport manager who effectively changed the face of London. Joining the Underground in 1906 he rose to become managing director in the 1920s and was chief executive of London Transport in 1933–40. See Oliver Green, 'Appearance Values: Frank Pick and the Art of London Transport', in David Bownes and Oliver Green (eds), *London Transport Posters*, Lund Humphries/London Transport Museum, London, 2008.

11. Tony Sarg (1880–1942) was a German-American painter, illustrator and caricaturist who designed a total of 32 posters for the London Underground between 1912 and 1914 before moving to the United States with his family after the start of the First World War.

12. For a comprehensive account of early British aviation see Graham Smith, *Taking to the Skies*, Countryside Books, Newbury, 2003.

13. Charles Rolls (1877–1910) had formed his well-known partnership with Henry Royce (1863–1933) in 1906, two years after their famous mutual introduction at the Midland Hotel, Manchester. Rolls provided the financial backing and business acumen to complement Royce's technical expertise in Rolls-Royce branded motor car production. When Rolls took up flying in 1907 he tried to persuade Royce to design an aero engine, but the first Rolls-Royce engines for aircraft were not produced until 1914, after Rolls' death. In the long term, Rolls-Royce aero engines were to be a far more successful business venture than luxury car production.

14. The Schneider Trophy has stayed permanently in Britain since 1931 under the rules of the contest, following the third successive competition win by a British pilot. It can now be seen on display in the Science Museum, London.

15. For a wider, international perspective on the culture of aviation as it developed in the early twentieth century, see Robert Wohl, *The Spectacle of Flight: Aviation and the Western Imagination, 1920–1950*, Yale University Press, New Haven, CT, and London, 2005, and Scott W. Palmer, *Dictatorship of the Air: Aviation Culture and the Fate of Modern Russia*, Cambridge University Press, Cambridge, 2006.

16. Igor Sikorsky (1889–1972) was a Russian-born pioneer of aviation in both helicopters and fixed wing aircraft. He emigrated to the United States in 1919, founded the Sikorsky Aircraft Corporation in 1923 and developed the first of Pan American Airways' ocean-conquering flying boats in the 1930s.

17. See R.E.G. (Ron) Davies, *British Airways: An Airline and Its Aircraft. Volume 1 1919–1939, The Imperial Years*, Paladwr Press, McLean, VA, 2005.

18. International aviation meets and competitions had been held in Austria, Belgium, France, Germany, Great Britain, Italy and even Egypt, as well as the United States, in the five years before the outbreak of war. See Henry Serrano Villard and Willis M. Allen, Jr, *Looping the Loop: Posters of Flight*, Kales Press, San Diego, CA, 2000, plate 67. This beautifully produced book was published in conjunction with an exhibition of early aviation posters organised by the National Air and Space Museum, the Allen Airways Flying Museum and the Smithsonian Institution Travelling Exhibition Service.

19. Alcock and Brown's wrecked plane was put back together again by Vickers, who had built it, and Rolls-Royce, who supplied the twin engines. The aircraft was presented to the Science Museum in London where it is still on permanent display.

20. Hansard, 11 March 1920, quoted in Robert Bluffield *Imperial Airways – The Birth of the British Airline Industry 1914–1940*, Ian Allan Hersham, 2009, p.15.

21. Handley Page, Instone, Daimler Airway (which had acquired AT&T) and the British Marine Air Navigation Co., which pioneered flying boat services from Southampton.

22. For a concise account of the years preceding the creation of Imperial Airways, see H.J. Dyos and D.H. Aldcroft, *British Transport, An Economic Survey from the Seventeenth Century to the Twentieth*, Penguin, Harmondsworth, 1974, pp.400–407.

23. At the 1923 grouping, four large private companies took over from 120 companies of various sizes. These were the Great Western Railway (GWR), London Midland & Scottish Railway (LMSR), London & North Eastern Railway (LNER) and Southern Railway (SR), all of which were nationalised in 1948 to create British Railways (BR), later to be privatised in 1994–7.

24. Frank Searle (1874–1948) is best known for his pre-aviation engineering achievement in designing the B-type motor bus for the London General Omnibus Company in 1910. This was London's first reliable, mass-produced bus, as important to urban public transport development in Britain as Henry Ford's Model T was to private motoring in the United States.

25. George Woods Humphery was a former engineer and Royal Flying Corps pilot. As managing director of Imperial he was apparently competent but abrasive. Staff relations were never good. Woods Humphery was severely criticised in the Cadman Report of 1938 for his management style but he was given no opportunity to defend himself. He resigned soon afterwards just as John Reith arrived as the new full-time chairman. They already knew each other well. In fact, Woods Humphery had been best man at Reith's wedding, but he was not asked to reconsider his resignation and stay on at Imperial.

Reith was shocked to find Imperial a one-man band with no effective management structure in place. He later wrote in his autobiography, 'when I left the BBC no one need have noticed it. Without Woods Humphery, no one in Imperial Airways knew where they were'. John Reith, *Into the Wind*, Hodder and Stoughton, London, 1949.

26. Quoted in A.S. Jackson, *Imperial Airways and the First British Airlines 1919–40*, Terence Dalton, Lavenham, 1990. Jackson gives a well-informed and perceptive account of Imperial's internal conflicts and dysfunctional management.

27. Quoted in Jackson 1990, p.34.

28. Quoted in Stedman S. Hanks, *International Airports*, Ronald Press, New York, NY, 1929. American author Hanks considered Croydon and Berlin Templehof the best airports in the world at this time, far superior to anything in the United States.

29. Sir Eric Geddes's speech, first AGM of Imperial Airways Ltd, reported in 'Company Meetings', *The Times*, 30 December 1925.

30. For explorations of the changing attitude towards the Empire in Britain between the wars, see John MacKenzie (ed.), *Imperialism and Popular Culture*, Manchester University Press, Manchester, 1986, and Denis Judd, *Empire: The British Imperial Experience from 1765 to the Present*, Harper Collins, London, 1996.

31. See Stephen Constantine, *Buy and Build, The Advertising Posters of the Empire Marketing Board*, PRO, London, 1986, and Melanie Horton, *Empire Marketing Board Posters*, Manchester Art Galleries/ Scala Publishers, London, 2010.

32. See Note 25 above.

33. Commercial airship development still looked promising at this time and was part of government strategy by 1926. The two large prototype British airships built for long-distance Empire service, R100 and R101, were both completed in 1929–30. On its maiden flight to Delhi in October 1930 R101 crashed in France, killing nearly everyone on board. The victims included Sir Sefton Brancker and the new Air Minister, Lord Thompson. Britain's airship programme died with them.

34. Sir Sefton Brancker, *Imperial Communications, Journal of the Proceedings of the Institute of Transport*, November 1924, pp.51–8.

35. Alan Cobham, *Australia and Back*, A. & C. Black, London, 1927.

36. Geoffrey de Havilland set up his own aircraft company in 1920 when George Holt Thomas sold Airco, the company for which he was chief designer, to the Birmingham Small Arms Company. The de Havilland Aircraft Company was based at Stag Lane Aerodrome near Edgware, moving to Hatfield in the 1930s.

37. For an account of the *Flying Scotsman* race, an example of Imperial's rather ham-fisted public relations at this time, see Jackson 1990, p.38.

38. See the first two volumes of the comprehensive three-volume history: Bob Learmonth, Joanna Nash and Douglas Cluett, *The First Croydon Airport 1915–1928*, London Borough of Sutton, London, 1977; and Bob Learmonth, Joanna Nash and Douglas Cluett, *Croydon Airport 1928–1939, The Great Days*, London Borough of Sutton, London, 1980.

39. Quoted in Learmonth, Nash and Cluett 1977.

40. *The Times*, 3 May 1928.

41. Quoted in Smith 2003, p.194.

42. See David Luff, *Amy Johnson: Enigma in the Sky*, Airlife, Shrewsbury, 2002. Johnson is the best known of many women who became skilled pilots in the inter-war years, though none of them were allowed to fly passenger aircraft at the time. Amy's trusty DH.60, *Jason*, is preserved in the Science Museum, London.

43. *Wallington and Carshalton Times*, 7 August 1930.

44. Heathrow, London's principal airport from 1946, had no direct rail service until 1977, when an extension of the Piccadilly line was opened to link it to central London.

45. For international comparisons, see Hugh Pearman, *Airports: A Century of Architecture*, Laurence King, London, 2004.

46. Imperial Airways passengers travelling to or from central London were transferred by car. The nearest railway station to the airport was at Waddon, on a Southern Railway branch line with no fast and direct service to London.

47. Harry Harper and Robert Brenard, *The Romance of the Flying Mail: A Pageant of Aerial Progress*, Routledge, London, 1932.

48. See Arthur W.J.G. Ord-Hume, *Imperial Airways from Early Days to BOAC*, Stenlake, Catrine, 2010, for an evocative, knowledgeable and superbly illustrated account of Imperial's operations and aircraft.

49. C.F. Snowden Gamble (1895–1940) was an RAF lieutenant in the First World War and wrote a study of the military use of the air called *The Air Arm* which became a standard work. He was a forest engineer in Burma before joining Imperial Airways and becoming its publicity manager in 1931. Called up in August 1939 he returned to the RAF as a squadron leader but died suddenly in April 1940 at the age of 45. An obituary in the *British Airways Newsletter* described him as having 'died as he lived, overworking wholeheartedly and hopefully for the nation and aviation'.

50. Stuarts was founded in 1922 by H. Stuart Menzies, a talented copywriter. It was a small agency that built a reputation for its innovative and high-class advertising campaigns for select and quintessentially British companies such as Fortnum & Mason and Keiller's marmalade.

51. J.R.M. (Marcus) Brumwell (1901–83) joined Stuarts in 1924 and became the agency's main link with the art world while Menzies concentrated on written copy. Initially this was through Brumwell's friendship with a group of young modern artists that included Ben Nicholson, Barbara Hepworth and Henry Moore. He became a partner in Stuarts when Menzies retired in 1938 and was a co-founder of the Design Research Unit (DRU) design consultancy in 1942.

52. Quoted in Joe Brumwell, *Bright Ties, Bold Ideas*, The Tie Press, Truro, 2010, a tribute by his son to Marcus Brumwell's life and influential work in advertising and design.

53. 'Modern Industry and its Advertising – Imperial Airways', *Commercial Art & Industry*, February 1933, pp.75–80.

54. Theyre Lee-Elliott (1903–88) was a graphic designer and artist who became an authority on the ballet. The Speedbird, commissioned by Stuarts for Imperial, is his most significant work, the original designs for which he left to the Victoria and Albert Museum.

55. As Note 53 above.

56. Theyre Lee-Elliot interviewed by *BOAC News*, January 18, 1963

57. The evolution and significance of the 'Flight' poster and Kauffer's huge influence on poster art are well described in Mark Haworth-Booth, *E. McKnight Kauffer, A Designer and His Public*, V&A Publications, London, 2005.

58. Quoted in Sir Francis Meynell, 'An Appreciation', *E. McKnight Kauffer Memorial Exhibition*, exh. cat., Victoria and Albert Museum, London, 1955.

59. E. McKnight Kauffer, 'The Poster and Symbolism', in William Gamble (ed.), *Penrose's Annual 1924: The Process Year Book and Review of the Graphic Arts*, Percy Lund Humphries, London, 1924, p.44, quoted by Alexandra Harris in *The Poster King*, exh.cat., Estorick Collection, London, 2011. This booklet reproduces a report from *Commercial Art* magazine, December 1923, of a debate at the Art Workers Guild in London about 'The Present Day Poster' where Kauffer clashed with the advertising manager of Pears' Soap.

60. See Alexandra Harris, *Romantic Moderns: English Writers, Artists and the Imagination from Virginia Woolf to John Piper*, Thames & Hudson, London, 2010.

61. POST 33/2 912A file, British Postal Museum & Archive, London.

62. Imperial Airways pamphlet, 1937, BA Heritage Centre archives. See also Frances Spalding, *John Piper, Myfanwy Piper: Lives in Art*, Oxford University Press, Oxford, 2009, p.86.

63. See essays by Nikolaus Pevsner on both Pick and the DIA reprinted in Nikolaus Pevsner, *Studies in Art, Architecture and Design: Volume 2 Victorian and After*, Thames & Hudson, London, 1968.

64. For a concise and perceptive assessment, see Ruth Artmonsky, *Jack Beddington, The Footnote Man*, Artmonsky Arts, London, 2006.

65. See *The Shell Poster Book*, Profile Books, London, 1998.

66. See Artmonsky 2006, pp.67–71.

67. See Paul Rennie, *Design: GPO Posters*, Antique Collectors' Club, Woodbridge, 2011.

68. This commentary on Imperial's films is adapted from Scott Anthony, 'The public education programmes of Imperial Airways: Aviation and the British imagination between the wars', lecture to the Maitland Society, Downing College, Cambridge, 29 November 2011.

69. Quoted from Donald Taylor, 'Official Publicity (Letters to the Editor)', *The Times*, 18 April 1944, p.5.

70. C.F. Snowden Gamble speaking at premier of new films about Imperial Airways, *Imperial Airways Gazette*, September 1937, BA Heritage Collection.

71. See Scott Anthony, 'The Future's in the Air: Imperial Airways and the British Documentary Film Movement', *Journal of British Film and Television*, vol.8, no.3, 2011.

72. 'The Work of Edward Bawden, Designer and Illustrator *Art and Industry*, vol.22, 1937. See also Caroline Bacon and James McGregor, *Edward Bawden*, Cecil Higgins Art Gallery, Bedford, 2008.

73. Rex Whistler's archive, including an original sketch for the Imperial coronation poster, is now held by Salisbury Museum. See the catalogues, writings and biography by his artist brother, Laurence Whistler, *The Laughter and the Urn: The Life of Rex Whistler*, Weidenfeld & Nicolson, London, 1986.

74. See 'Obituary: James Gardner', *Independent*, 29 March 1995, by fellow designer Sir Hugh Casson.

75. Herbert Read, 'Foreword', *Flying over the Empire*, exh.cat., Gieves Gallery, Old Bond Street, London, 9–21 July 1934, printed for Imperial Airways by the Curwen Press, London, BA Heritage Collection.

76. All statistics are quoted from Dyos and Aldcroft 1974, p.413.

77. Not to be confused with modern British Airways (BA), which was established as the national carrier through the merger of BOAC and BEA in 1974. This British Airways was privatised in 1986.

78. When Prime Minister Neville Chamberlain made his three visits to Germany to negotiate with Hitler in September 1938, and returned brandishing his infamous 'piece of paper' agreement signed in Munich, he flew from Heston in a brand new British Airways Electra airliner.

79. See Adrian B. Rance (ed.), *Seaplanes and Flying Boats of the Solent*, Southampton University, Southampton, 1981, and Peter London, *British Flying Boats*, The History Press, Sutton, 2011.

80. Quoted from a perceptive essay by Adrian Smith, 'A Vision Unfulfilled: Southampton's ambition for the world's first sea aerodrome', in Miles Taylor (ed.), *Southampton, Gateway to the British Empire*, I.B. Taurus, London, 2007.

81. 'The Cadman Report', Government Command Paper 5685-1938.

82. Charles Mowat, *Britain between the Wars*, University of Chicago Press, Chicago, IL, 1961, quoted by Dyos and Aldcroft 1974, p.417.

Conflict and a Changing World
Oliver Green

83. Kenneth Holmes, 'Design for Air Travel Service', Special BOAC issue, *Art & Industry*, May 1947.

Queen and Comet: Art and Aviation in the New Elizabethan Age *Scott Anthony*

84. 'Elizabethans '52', reprinted in *BOAC Magazine*, April 1952, p.4.

85. Quoted in Ben Pimlott, *The Queen: Elizabeth II and the Monarchy*, Harper Collins, London, 2002, p.193.

86. See Kenneth Munson, *Pictorial History of BOAC and Imperial Airways*, Ian Allan, London, 1970.

87. K. Holmes, 'Design for Air Travel Service', *Art & Industry*, May 1947, p.144.

88. See Henry Hessner, *Camera at War*, Jarrolds, London, 1943; Henry Hessner, *Comet Highway*, John Murray, London, 1953.

89. 'Latest Livery Means Cooler Customers', *BOAC Magazine*, December 1950, p.5.

90. See Catherine Moriarty, June Rose and Naomi Games, *Abram Games: His Life and Work*, Princeton Architectural Press, New York, NY, 2003.

91. Abram Games, *Over My Shoulder*, Studio Books, London, 1960, p.4.

92. See Mary Banham and Bevis Hillier (eds), *A Tonic to the Nation: The Festival of Britain, 1951*, Thames & Hudson, London, 1976; and Becky E. Conekin, *The Autobiography of a Nation: The 1951 Festival of Britain*, Manchester University Press, Manchester, 2000.

93. 'Meet your Waterloo', *BEA Magazine*, May 1953, p.10.

94. Games 1960, p.12.

95. Games 1960, p.6.

96. 'Every Ninth Passenger An Animal', *BOAC Magazine*, December 1950, p.4; see also 'Even Birds Fly By BOAC', *BOAC Magazine*, December 1952, p.2.

97. 'Thoughts on Leaving BOAC', *BOAC Magazine*, September 1950, p.7.

98. Quoted in Nigel Fountain, 'The Wrong Stuff', *Guardian*, 28 September 1996, p.32.

99. See James Hamilton-Paterson, *Empire of the Clouds: When Britain's Aircraft Ruled the World*, Faber & Faber, London, 2010.

100. 'By "Comet" to Johannesburg', *Pathé Newsreel*, 21 April 1952.

101. 'Comets and Transatlantic Psychology', *Flight*, 12 February 1954, p.176; F. Jackson, 'The New Air Age: BOAC and Design Policy, 1945–1960', *Journal of Design History*, vol.3, no.4, 1991, pp.167–85.

102. Quoted in Fountain 1996.

103. 'Fun for the CD1 – BEA advertises', *BEA Magazine*, February 1957, p.2.

104. *BEA Magazine*, February 1957.

105. 'And in retrospect', *BEA Magazine*, May 1952, p.12.

106. 'Air Travel? You Ain't Seen Nothing Yet!', *BOAC Magazine*, January 1960, p.12.

107. 'Far Away Places: The story of Cyprus Airways', *BEA Magazine*, June 1949, p.4.

108. See Nicholas Bullock, *Building the Post-War World: Modern Architecture and Reconstruction in Britain*, Routledge, London, 2002.

109. Quoted in John R. Gold, *The Practice of Modernism: Modern Architects and Urban Transformation, 1954–1972*, Routledge, Abingdon and New York, 2007, p.45.

110. Interview with Mary de Saulles, 12 September 2011.

111. 'Prototype of a PRO', *BEA Magazine*, March 1960, p.7.

112. 'Focus on Europe', *BOAC Review*, March 1961, p.14.

113. Quoted in Alan Gallop, *Time Flies – Heathrow at 60*, The History Press, Sutton, 2005, p.77.

114. See Basil Smallpeice, *Of Comets and Queens: An Autobiography*, Airlife, London, 1981.

115. The passenger appeal of the VC-10 did not save it. All the Standard VC-10s were withdrawn from use in 1974 after only ten years' service. BOAC decided they were no longer economically viable and 747 jumbo jets took over. The Super VC-10s survived in BA service until 1981. Ironically most of them had a long afterlife with the RAF, which continues to operate a few from Brize Norton in Oxfordshire. The ever-popular VC-10 even has its own fan website, www. vc10.net.

116. 'The Motown Invasion', BBC Radio 2, 5 April 2005.

117. 'Sales Training Centre at Old Burlington Street', *BOAC Magazine*, October 1960, p.13.

118. 'British Men Are So Dashing!', *BOAC Magazine*, October 1960, p.21.

119. 'How fashions change', *BOAC News*, 6 September 1967, p.5.

120. 'We Had to Kill the Stewardess', *BEA Magazine*, September 1947, p.12.

121. Fiona MacCarthy, 'Obituary: Robin Day: Celebrated furniture designer', *Guardian*, 18 November 2010, p.42.

122. Quoted in Lesley Jackson, *Robin and Lucienne Day: Pioneers of Contemporary Design*, Mitchell Beazley, London, 2001, p.138.

123. M. Hope, F.H.K. Henrion interview (video clip), FHK Henrion Archive and Research Library, University of Brighton, 1989; D. Preston, 'The Corporate trailblazers', *Ultrabold: The Journal of St Bride Library*, no.10, Summer 2011, pp.14–21.

Epilogue

124. Quoted in Le Corbusier 1935.

125. Entry of 5 September 1942 in Charles Lindbergh, *The War Time Journals of Charles A. Lindbergh*, Harcourt Brace Jovanovich, New York, 1970, pp.706–8; Wohl 2005, p.319.

Timeline

1903
First powered flight in the world achieved by the Wright brothers at Kitty Hawk, USA.

1908
First powered flight in Britain made by American Samuel F. Cody at Aldershot. Nearby Brooklands becomes a pioneering aviation centre.

1909
First successful flight across the English Channel by Frenchman Louis Blériot, from Calais to Dover. First aero exhibition at Olympia, London, and first aviation races in England at Doncaster and Blackpool.

1910
First London aerodrome opened at Hendon by Claude Grahame-White. Frenchman Louis Paulhan beats Grahame-White in the race to be first to fly from London to Manchester in 24 hours.

Charles Rolls is the first person in Britain to be killed in an aero accident, at an international aviation meeting at Bournemouth.

1911
First airmail service demonstration in Britain by Grahame-White Company, making special postal deliveries from Hendon to Windsor Castle for the coronation celebrations of King George V.

1914–18
First World War. No civil aviation in Europe, but rapid military progress in aircraft design.

1919
First scheduled civil air services from London to Paris and Brussels. Air Transport & Travel flew from Hounslow and Handley Page from Cricklewood, using converted military bomber aircraft.

1920
Croydon becomes the principal 'air station' for London.

1923
First British flying boat service from Southampton (Woolston) to St Peter Port, Guernsey, by British Marine Air Navigation (BMAN).

1924
Foundation of Imperial Airways as single, subsidised national airline for Britain through merger of BMAN, Daimler Hire, Handley Page and Instone. Alan Cobham makes first aerial survey trip for an Imperial route to India, carrying Air Minister Sir Sefton Brancker.

1926
Imperial's first purpose-built airliner, the Armstrong Whitworth Argosy, introduced on London (Croydon) to Paris (Le Bourget) service.

1927
Imperial takes over the RAF Desert Air Mail service from Cairo to Baghdad, its first long-distance service in the Middle East, soon extended to Karachi and Delhi.

Silver Wing full-catering service introduced by Imperial on its main European service from London to Paris.

1928
New passenger terminal and control tower opens at Croydon Airport, 'the most perfectly equipped in the world'.

1930
R101 airship crashes in France on maiden flight to India, ending British airship development programme.

1931
Handley Page HP42, the largest airliner in the world, enters Imperial service on London–Paris and empire routes.

Bill Snowden Gamble becomes publicity manager for Imperial and appoints Stuarts as advertising agents, led by Marcus Brumwell.

1932
Theyre Lee-Elliott designs Speedbird, a dynamic new graphic symbol for Imperial Airways, commissioned by Stuarts.

Imperial introduces first Cape to Cairo service through Africa, using both flying boats and landplanes.

1933
Imperial's first monoplane airliner, the Atalanta, introduced on African routes.

1934
Imperial opens first airmail service from London to Australia, the longest airline route in the world, in conjunction with Indian Trans-Continental and Qantas Empire Airways.

British government announces the Empire Air Mail Scheme. Imperial orders 28 large, modern flying boats to operate the principal empire routes.

1935
British Airways Limited (BAL) formed as private company to operate domestic and European services.

1936
First of Short C-class Empire Flying Boats delivered, soon to be Imperial's largest fleet of aircraft.

1937
BAL acquires American Lockheed Electra monoplanes.

Imperial introduces Empire Flying Boats on long-distance services, using Southampton as its seaplane base in Britain.

First North Atlantic survey flights.

1938
Imperial introduces the aerodynamic DH.91 Frobisher, the fastest airliner in the world and the first to carry the Speedbird symbol on the fuselage.

Munich crisis. Prime Minister Neville Chamberlain flies to Germany three times by BAL Electra to negotiate peace agreement with Hitler.

1939–40
Creation of British Overseas Airways Corporation (BOAC) through merger of Imperial and British Airways into a single national airline, operational from 1940 but on a restricted wartime basis.

1939–45
Second World War. Normal civil aviation suspended but BOAC operates passenger and transport services throughout the war under difficult and dangerous conditions.

1945
BOAC sets up a design committee to establish a strong 'house style' and harmonise every aspect of design including corporate identity, poster publicity, staff uniforms, aircraft liveries and interior décor.

1946
Heathrow opens to international traffic, replacing Croydon as the official London Airport but operating from temporary buildings.

British European Airways (BEA) created as second state-run carrier for domestic and European services. British South American Airways (BSAA) was also formed as the third state-run carrier for South American services.

BOAC introduces fully pressurised Lockheed Constellation airliner on its transatlantic service, with uniformed stewardesses as cabin crew.

1949
BOAC introduces luxurious double deck Boeing Stratocruisers on London–New York service via Prestwick.

1950
BEA puts first Vickers Viscount turbo-prop into service from Northolt to Paris and starts first scheduled passenger helicopter services on domestic routes. BOAC ends flying boat operation from Southampton.

1951
Festival of Britain.

1952
BOAC introduces DH Comet, the world's first jet airliner, on its Heathrow to Johannesburg service.

1953
Coronation of Queen Elizabeth II.

1953–54
Three Comet 1 crash disasters.

1955
BEA introduces London Waterloo to Heathrow helicopter service. Opening of Heathrow's first terminal, the Queen's Building.

1958
BOAC introduces first transatlantic jet service using the Comet 4. BEA Ambassador crash at Munich airport. Among the dead are members of the Manchester United football team returning from Belgrade.

1960
BOAC starts using American Boeing 707 with British Rolls-Royce jet engines on Heathrow to New York services.

1964
BOAC introduces Vickers VC-10 on its Heathrow to Lagos service. BEA introduces DH Trident on London to Copenhagen service.

1966
Freddie Laker starts Laker Airways, the first of the 'no-frills' airlines.

1970
British Caledonian created by the Government as a commercial 'second force' in British aviation.

1971
BOAC operates its first commercial Boeing 747 'Jumbo jet' flight from Heathrow to New York (JFK).

1972
Airbus launch successful A300 aircraft.

1974
British Airways (BA) created through merger of BOAC and BEA.

1976
First scheduled supersonic BA flights with Concorde introduced from Heathrow to Bahrain.

1977
Opening of first rail link to Heathrow, an extension of London Underground's Piccadilly line.

1978
American Airlines challenge the International Air Transport Association's role in price-setting, marking a move away from post-war economics to a new era of deregulation.

1984
BA introduces new livery designed by Landor Associates of California, in preparation for privatisation, which includes replacing the 1932 Speedbird symbol with the Speedwing.

Creation of Virgin Atlantic.

1987
BA privatised by the Conservative government.

1989
BA's 'World's Favourite Airline' slogan introduced in iconic television advertisement directed by Hugh Hudson with the 'smiling world face' made up of people and a soundtrack of Delibes' 'Flower Duet' music, associated with BA ever since.

1997
BA unveils a new livery and corporate identity design by Newell and Sorrell, which features the Speedmarque, a replacement for the Speedwing. More controversially, each BA aircraft except Concorde, which is adorned with a new version of the union flag, is given a unique artist-designed tailplane to represent one of the countries served by BA worldwide.

1998
BA opens new international head office complex, the Waterside Building, at Harmondsworth, near Heathrow, designed by architects Niels Torp.

1999
British Airways London Eye officially opened by Prime Minister Tony Blair.

2001
Single European Sky initiative begins, starting the process of merging national airspaces into a single European airspace that integrates civil and military air traffic control.

2003
Last BA Concorde flight.

2005
Airbus A380, the world's largest passenger airplane, makes maiden flight. Airbus is the European aerospace rival to American giant Boeing, with production sites in France, Germany, the United Kingdom and Spain. It now produces more than 50 percent of the world's jet airliners.

2007
Signing of EU-US Open Skies agreement, allowing any airline of the European Union and any airline of the United States to fly between any point in the EU and any point in the US.

First Airbus A380 enters service with Singapore Airlines. British Airways orders 12 to be delivered from 2013

2008
Opening of Heathrow Terminal 5, the main base for BA international services.

2011
BA merges with Iberia to create the International Airlines Group (IAG) but retains its separate identity.

Selected Further Reading

This is not a comprehensive reading list but includes most of the secondary sources that we found useful in the preparation of this book. Many of these publications are now out of print and only available in specialist libraries or for second-hand purchase. The list covers primarily the development of British civil aviation and its promotion through posters and other visual publicity such as film from the early 1900s to the 1960s. We have included some relevant contextual works on applied art and design, and on international civil aviation in this period, but excluded even the tip of the vast iceberg of material on military aviation history and studies of aircraft design and technology, which are well beyond our areas of expertise.

Art and Design

Scott Anthony and James G. Mansell (eds), *The Projection of Britain: A History of the GPO Film Unit*, BFI, London, 2011

Ruth Artmonsky and Brian Webb, *Design: FHK Henrion*, Antique Collectors' Club, Woodbridge, 2011

Caroline Bacon and James McGregor, *Edward Bawden*, Cecil Higgins Art Gallery, Bedford, 2008

David Bernstein, introduction, '*That's Shell – that is!', An Exhibition of Shell Advertising Art*, Barbican Art Gallery and Shell UK, London, 1983

David Bownes and Oliver Green (eds), *London Transport Posters, A Century of Art and Design*, London Transport Museum/Lund Humphries, London, 2008

Louis-Jean Calvet and Philippe-Michel Thibault, *Air France*

Posters. Making the World Dream, Le Cherche Midi, Paris, 2006

Beverley Cole and Richard Durack, *Railway Posters, 1923–1947*, Laurence King, London, 1992

Colin Cruddas, *100 Years of Advertising in British Aviation*, The History Press, Stroud, 2008

Stephen Constantine, *Buy and Build: The Advertising Posters of the Empire Marketing Board*, HMSO, London, 1986

Peter Delius and Jacek Slaski (eds), *Airline Design*, TeNeues, Düsseldorf, 2005

Naomi Games, Catherine Moriarty and June Rose, *Abram Games, Graphic Designer: Maximum Meaning, Minimum Means*, Lund Humphries, London, 2003

Oliver Green, *Underground Art: London Transport Posters from 1908 to the Present*, London Transport Museum/Laurence King, London, 2000

L.D. Guell (ed.), *Iberia mil fotos para la historia 1927–2001*, Tauro Editiones, Madrid, 2001

Mark Haworth-Booth, *E. McKnight Kauffer: A Designer and His Public*, V&A Publications, London, 2005

Edward McKnight Kauffer, *The Art of the Poster: Its Origin, Evolution and Purpose*, Cecil Palmer, London, 1924

Don Middleton, *British Aviation: A Design History*, Ian Allan, Shepperton, 1986

Jan Morris, introduction, *Riding the Skies, Classic Posters from the Golden Age of Flying*, Bloomsbury, London, 1989

Hugh Pearman, *Airports, A Century of Architecture*, Laurence King, London, 2004

Paul Rennie, *Modern British Posters, Art, Design and Communication*, Black Dog, London, 2010

Paul Rennie, *Design: GPO Posters*,

Antique Collectors' Club, Woodbridge, 2011

G. Szurovy, *The Art of the Airways*, MBI, St Paul, MN, 2002

Robert Taylor, *The Aviation Art of Frank Wootton*, David & Charles, Newton Abbot, 2005

Margaret Timmers, *A Century of Olympic Games Posters*, V&A Publications, London, 2008

Margaret Timmers (ed.), *The Power of the Poster*, V&A Publications, London, 1998

Henry Serrano Villard and Willis M. Allen Jr, *Looping the Loop, Posters of Flight*, Kales Press, San Diego, CA, 2000

Geza Szurovy, *The Art of the Airways*, Zenith Press, Minneapolis, 2002

Alain Weill, *Graphics: A Century of Poster and Advertising Design*, Thames & Hudson, London, 2004

Robert Wohl, *A Passion for Wings: Aviation and the Western Imagination, 1908–1918*, Yale University Press, New Haven, CT, 1996

Robert Wohl, *The Spectacle of Flight: Aviation and the Western Imagination, 1920–1950*, Yale University Press, New Haven, CT, 2007

Stuart Wrede, *The Modern Poster*, Museum of Modern Art, New York, NY, 1988

Autobiography/Biography

Ruth Artmonsky, *Jack Beddington, The Footnote Man*, Artmonsky Arts, London, 2006

Christian Barman, *The Man Who Built London Transport: A Biography of Frank Pick*, David & Charles, Newton Abbot, 1979

Tom Bower, *Branson*, Fourth Estate, London, 2001

Alan Bramson, *Pure Luck: The*

Authorised Biography of Sir Thomas Sopwith, Crecy, Manchester, 2005

Joe Brumwell, *Bright Ties, Bold Ideas: Marcus Brumwell, Pioneer of C20 Advertising, Champion of the Artists,* The Tie Press, Truro, 2010

Sir Alan Cobham, *To the Ends of the Earth: Memoirs of a Pioneering Aviator,* Tempus, Stroud, 2007 (first published 1927)

Sir Alan Cobham, *Twenty-thousand Miles in a Flying Boat,* Tempus, Stroud, 2007 (first published 1930)

Sholto Douglas, *Years of Command: A Personal Story*, Collins, London, 1966

Roger Eglin and Berry Ritchie, *Fly Me, I'm Freddie*, Weidenfeld & Nicolson, London, 1980

Claude Grahame-White, *Flying: An Epitome and a Forecast*, Chatto & Windus, London, 1930

Sir Geoffrey de Havilland, *Sky Fever*, Hamish Hamilton, London, 1961

Garry Jenkins, *'Colonel' Cody and the Flying Cathedral: The Adventures of the Cowboy that Conquered Britain's Skies,* Simon & Schuster, New York, NY, 1999

David Luff, *Amy Johnson: Enigma in the Sky*, Airlife, Shresbury, 2002

Sir Peter Masefield, with Bill Gunston, *Flight Path: The Autobiography of Sir Peter Masefield*, Airlife, Shrewsbury, 2002

Gordon P. Olley, *A Million Miles in the Air*, Hodder & Stoughton, London, 1934

Lord Reith, *Into the Wind*, Hodder & Stoughton, London, 1949

Sir Basil Smallpiece, *Of Comets and Queens*, Airlife, Shrewsbury, 1981

Viscount Templewood (Sir Samuel Hoare), *Empire of the Air: The Advent of the Air Age, 1922–*

1929, Collins, London, 1957

Lowell Thomas, *European Skyways: The Story of a Tour of Europe by Airplane*, Riverside Press, Cambridge, MA, 1927

Sir Miles Thomas, *Out on a Wing*, Michael Joseph, London, 1964

Sir Adam Thompson, *High Risk: The Politics of the Air*, Sidgwick & Jackson, London, 1990

James Tobin, *To Conquer the Air, The Wright Brothers and the Great Race for Flight*, Free Press, New York and London, 2003

Sir Alliott Verdon-Roe, *The World of Wings and Things*, Hurst & Blackwell, London, 1939

Graham Wallace, *Claude Graham-White,* Putnam, London, 1960

History

Philip Bagwell and Peter Lyth, *Transport in Britain, from Canal Lock to Gridlock*, Hambledon & London, London, 2002

John Batchelor and Malcolm V. Lowe, *The Complete Encyclopedia of Flight 1848–1939*, Rebo International, Lisse, 2006

David Beaty, *The Story of Transatlantic Flight*, Airlife, Shrewsbury, 2003 (originally published 1976)

Robert Bluffield, *Imperial Airways: The Birth of the British Airline Industry, 1914–1940*, Ian Allan, Hersham, 2009

Winston Bray, *The History of BOAC, 1939–1974*, Wessex Press, Camberley, 1974

R.E.G. Davies, *British Airways, An Airline and its Aircraft, Vol. 1: 1919–1939, The Imperial Years*, Paladwr Press, 2005

Peter J. Davis, *East African: An Airline Story*, Runnymeade, Egham, 1993

Gunter G. Endres, *British Civil Aviation*, Ian Allan, Shepperton, 1985

Libbie Escolme-Schmidt, *Glamour in the Skies: The Golden Age of the Air Stewardess*, The History Press, Stroud, 2009

Alexander Frater, *The Balloon Factory, The Story of the Men Who Built Britain's First Flying Machines*, Picador, London, 2008

Charles H. Gibbs-Smith, *The Aeroplane: An Historical Survey of its Origins and Development*, HMSO, London, 1960

Richard P. Hallion, *Taking Flight: Inventing the Aerial Age from Antiquity through the First World War*, Oxford University Press, Oxford, 2000

James Hamilton-Paterson, *Empire of the Clouds: When Britain's Aircraft Ruled the World*, Faber and Faber, London, 2010

Harry Harper, *The Romance of a Modern Airway,* Sampson Low, London, 1930

Harry Harper and Robert Brenard, *The Romance of the Flying Mail,* Routledge, London, 1933

Brian Harris, *Babs, Beacon and Boadicea: A History of Computing in British Airways and its Predecessor Airlines*, Speedwing Press, Hounslow, 1993

Kenneth Hudson, *Air Travel: A Social History,* Adams & Dart, Bath, 1973

Robert Jackson, *The Sky Their Frontier, The Story of the World's Pioneer Airlines and Routes 1920–1940*, Airlife Publishing, Shrewsbury, 1983

Howard Johnson, *Wings over Brooklands: The Birthplace of British Aviation*, Whittet Books, 1981

Bob Learmonth, Joanna Nash and Douglas Cluett, *Croydon Airport 1928–1939, The Great Days*, London Borough of Sutton, London, 1980

Bob Learmonth, Joanna Nash and Douglas Cluett, *The First Croydon Airport 1915–1928*, London Borough of Sutton, London, 1977

Phil Lo Bao, *An Illustrated History of British European Airways,* Browncom Group, Feltham, 1989

Peter London, *British Flying Boats,* The History Press, Stroud, 2011

C. Martin-Sharp, *D.H: A History of de Havilland,* Airlife, Shrewsbury, 1960

Garry May, *The Challenge of BEA: The Story of a Great Airline's First 25 Years*, Oxley Press, London and Edinburgh, 1971

Kenneth Munson, *A Pictorial History of BOAC and Imperial Airways,* Ian Allan, Shepperton, 1970

Kenneth Munson, *Civil Aircraft of Yesteryear,* Ian Allan, Shepperton, 1967

Andrew Nahum, *Flying Machine,* Dorling Kindersley Eyewitness Guides, London, 1990

Joseph L. Nayler and Ernest Ower, *Flight Today,* Oxford University Press, Oxford, 1937

David Oliver, *Hendon Aerodrome: A History,* Airlife, Shrewsbury, 1994

Arthur W.J.G. Ord-Hume, *Imperial Airways from Early Days to BOAC*, Stenlake, Catrine, 2010

Susan Ottaway and Ian Ottoway, *Fly with the Stars: British South American Airways,* Sutton, Stroud, 2007

Harald J. Penrose, *Wings Across the World: An Illustrated History of British Airways,* Cassell, London, 1980

Gordon Pirie, *Air Empire: British Imperial Aviation, 1919–39,* Manchester University Press, Manchester, 2009

John Pudney, *The Seven Skies,* Putnam, London, 1959

Tom Quinn, *Wings Over the World: Tales from the Golden Age of Air Travel,* Aurum Press, London, 2003

Jay Rayner, *Star Dust Falling: The Story of the Plane that Vanished,* Doubleday, London, 2002

Arthur Reed, *Airline: The Inside Story of British Airways,* BBC Books, London, 1990

Ivan Rendall, *Reaching for the Skies: The Adventure of Flight,* BBC Books, London, 1988

Anthony Sampson, *Empires of the Sky: The Politics, Contests and Cartels of World Airlines,* Hodder & Stoughton, London, 1984

Graham Smith, *Taking to the Skies, The Story of British Aviation 1903–1939,* Countryside Books, Newbury, 2003

John Stroud, *Railway Air Services,* Ian Allan, Shepperton, 1987

John W.R. Taylor and Kenneth Munson (eds), *History of Aviation,* New English Library, London, 1978

Robert Wall, *Airliner,* New Burlington Books, London, 1980

Charles Woodley, *BOAC, An Illustrated History,* Tempus, Bristol, 2004

Charles Woodley, *Heathrow Airport, The First 25 Years,* The History Press, Stroud, 2010

Acknowledgements

This is not an official history of British Airways' illustrious predecessors, but we must thank Paul Jarvis, manager of the British Airways Heritage Collection, for commissioning the book and for his help and enthusiasm in seeing this project through. We are also grateful to archivist Jim Davies for his assistance and historical knowledge. They both made us very welcome on our visits to Waterside.

Gill Sparrow was immensely helpful in drawing together information on artists and designers in her capacity as a volunteer both for the Heritage Centre and at the Victoria and Albert Museum. Margaret Timmers of the Victoria and Albert Museum was closely involved at the start of this project, shared her expert knowledge of poster history and brought us together as authors. Scott Anthony would also like to thank Peter Mandler, Luke Heeley and Beryl Pong for their sage advice and astute additions, as well as the support of the Leverhulme Trust. We would also like to acknowledge the helpful support of Naomi Games, who now manages her father Abram's archive, Robin Ravilious for positive confirmation of her uncle Rex Whistler's work for Imperial, Charmain Pick for information about her late husband Beverley Pick's work for BOAC and BEA, and Mary de Saulles for her insightful personal recollections about the evolution of the red square and her other design work for BEA.

This book would not have been possible without the tenacity, creativity and diligence of everyone at Lund Humphries, particularly Lucy Clark, Miranda Harrison, Sarah Thorowgood and Cilla Kennedy. Many thanks too to our sympathetic editor Howard Watson and designer Heather Bowen.

British Airways Heritage Collection

When we started our research, the British Airways Heritage Collection was stored in a rather cramped hut at Heathrow, almost under the flight path at the end of a runway near Hatton Cross. In 2010 it was moved into Waterside, British Airways' impressive, modern, open-plan head office complex near Harmondsworth, just beyond the airport perimeter. Now housed in the new Speedbird Heritage Centre, it is right on the main interior 'street' of Waterside, and provides an attractive and inviting showcase for BA's latest developments in design and customer service as well as access to an important heritage collection stretching back over nine decades.

For us the posters are the stars of the British Airways Heritage Collection, but the collection also includes artworks, models, documents, uniforms, artefacts, film and photographs. A selection of posters, photographs and other material can be viewed online at www.britishairways.com/travel/history-and-heritage. Visitors to the Heritage Centre are welcome by appointment. Please contact British Airways Heritage Centre, Waterside, PO Box 365, Harmondsworth UB7 0GB, tel: 020 856 25777, www.baheritage.com.

Image Credits

Index